CANCER
and Your Pet

CANCER

and Your Pet

The Complete Guide to the Latest Research, Treatments, and Options

Debra M. Eldredge, DVM
and
Margaret H. Bonham
Foreword by Amy D. Shojai

Capital Ideas for Pets

CAPITAL
BOOKS, INC.
Sterling, Virginia

Capital Books, Inc.
P.O. Box 605
Herndon, Virginia 20172-0605

Book design and composition by Susan Mark
Coghill Composition Company
Richmond, Virginia

ISBN 1-931868-86-7 (alk.paper)

Library of Congress Cataloging-in-Publication Data

Eldredge, Debra.
    Cancer and your pet : the complete guide to the latest research, treatment, and options / by Debra M. Eldredge and Margaret H. Bonham ; foreword by Amy D. Shojai.—1st ed.
        p.   cm.
    Includes bibliographical references and index.
    ISBN 1-931868-86-7 (pbk. : alk. paper)
    1. Dogs—Diseases.   2. Cats—Diseases.   3. Cancer in animals.
4. Veterinary oncology.   I. Bonham, Margaret H.   II. Title.

SF992.C35E53   2005
636.7'0896994—dc22

                                                           2005010141

Printed in Canada on acid-free paper that meets the American National Standards Institute Z39-48 Standard.

First Edition

10   9   8   7   6   5   4   3   2   1

Deb would like to dedicate her contributions to this book to her beloved pets who have died of cancer over the years—Toby the English Setter, Wiley the Terv, Gus the Labrador Retriever, Bomber the TB mare, Venus de Milo the three-legged black cat, and all the beloved companions of my clients and friends.

Maggie would like to dedicate her contributions to her beloved pets who died of cancer over the years (Houston, Shadow, Conan, Skye, Spice, Mirin, and Kersel), but especially to Kiana who died in 2003 of osteosarcoma. Miss you, Hoot.

Acknowledgments

We would like to thank the many pets and their families who contributed to this book—Jane and Todd with Fang, Linda with Riser, Phyllis with Fred, Julie with Jordie, Dave and Vern with Tom, Sarah with Chase, Dusty with Chani, and Lin with Pepper. We'd like to that the Morris Animal Foundation, especially Heidi Jeter who put up with incessant questions from Maggie and really helped out. We'd like to thank Drs. Phillip Bergman, DVM, Ph.D., David Vail, DVM, and Carol Henry, DVM, for interviews. Thanks to Amy Shojai for the wonderful foreword.

Special thanks go to Beth Adelman, who helped solidify this project in Maggie's mind.

Thanks also to our families who had to forgo using the computer for long stretches and ate meals dodging books and articles on the kitchen table and generally putting up with our lack of time. Thanks to Larry, Maggie's husband, who offered moral support.

Special thanks to those pets who helped us—Samantha who kept Deb's computer functioning; Susan who supervised Deb and kept her on task; and Dani and Hokey who made Deb laugh; Haegl, Kira, and Kodiak who let Maggie know when it was time to do something else; and Hailey who kept Maggie's lap warm at 1:00 A.M. when everyone else was asleep.

Last, we'd like to thank Jessica Faust of Bookends for being a terrific agent.

Contents

Foreword

When we welcome cats and dogs into our lives, we anticipate years or even decades of shared joy. Over time, our bond grows ever stronger until life without our pet becomes difficult to imagine. Sadly, if a cat or dog lives long enough to enjoy this unparalleled communion, the chance increases that he or she may be stricken with cancer. There are exceptions, but aging pets most commonly fall victim to cancer.

Cancer. We whisper the word, fear it, and too often allow the idea to paralyze us. If you are reading this foreword, you love your pet and refuse to allow a scary word to control you or seal your pet's fate.

When your pet falls ill with cancer, you need expert guidance. To be helpful, information must be comprehensive, current, and correct. It must also be presented in an understandable and useful manner. Finally, such sensitive information demands a sincere and empathetic voice. *Cancer and Your Pet* fills these requirements with ease.

Authors Margaret Bonham and Debra Eldredge provide you with the tools you need to understand what you face and make informed decisions for the well-being of your special cats and dogs. They take you effortlessly through the complex subject, from demystifying the disease and discussing its various forms, to providing answers about potential treatment options, costs involved, and the decisions you'll face. Not every cancer or pet/owner partnership is the same. The book helps you evaluate options to choose the best path for *your* particular situation.

This is a book I hope you never need, but should never be without. Maggie and Deb provide a great service and resource to pet owners. I'm proud to be in the company of such fine pet writers. My copy will have a place of honor on my bookshelf.

Cancer and Your Pet helps you keep your cats and dogs happy and enjoying life throughout the diagnosis, treatment, and sometimes the final release into a loving pain-free death. Please know that whatever choice you ultimately make, when a decision comes out of love, *it cannot be wrong.* With this book as your guide, you and your pet won't be alone.

> —Amy D. Shojai, nationally known pet care and behavior authority, pet food industry consultant, and author of eighteen pet care titles, including *Complete Care for Your Aging Dog* and *Complete Care for Your Aging Cat.*

CANCER
and Your Pet

CHAPTER

1

Cancer in Pets[1]

IN THIS CHAPTER

- Learn what cancer is
- Learn what causes cancer
- Learn whether cancer is treatable
- Learn what myths surround cancer

Cancer. That word strikes fear into pet owners. Visions of hair loss, sickness, and death color our thoughts about cancer. Didn't Aunt Rose lose all her hair ten years ago when she was treated? Didn't the veterinarian recommend that we put Fluffy down when he got cancer five years ago? When faced with these anecdotes, you may look on your pet's prognosis as grim.

Nothing could be further from the truth. Cancer is the most treatable of chronic diseases. While cancer is indeed the number-one killer of pets over eight years old, as of this writing, a full 50 percent of all cancers are completely curable. Let us reiterate:

A full 50 percent of cancers are completely curable (42).

---

1. (From Sources 37,38, 39, 41,42,50,53, pages 211–215.)

Chase is a dog who has beaten the odds on cancer.

Case Study

In March 2003, Sarah Harrison received the dreaded news: her little Cocker–Springer Spaniel mix, Chase, had anal tumors and bladder cancer. He was just twelve years old at the time. Ms. Harrison, who lives in Denver, Colorado, took Chase to her vet for what she thought was an anal gland problem.

"Our vet told us it wasn't just impacted anal glands and sent us to the Veterinary Referral Center of Colorado [VRCC]," says Ms. Harrison.

The veterinarians at VRCC diagnosed anal tumors, and while they were using an ultrasound to determine how far the tumors had spread, they discovered the bladder cancer.

"I knew that bladder cancer was aggressive," says Ms. Harrison, "but the vets at VRCC gave me several options for treatment and the prognosis

for each. One option they gave me was to do nothing. Another option was surgery and chemotherapy. They also gave me the option of using radiation, but in Chase's case, they felt the chemotherapy and surgery was the best option."

Ms. Harrison had the veterinarians operate on Chase's tumors. After the surgery, Chase began an intensive treatment of chemotherapy consisting of a one- to two-hour session every three weeks for six months. "Chase didn't get sick after chemotherapy, although the surgery wiped him out," says Ms. Harrison. "After chemotherapy, he'd be bouncing around and was always hungry."

It has been a year since Chase was diagnosed with cancer. The veterinarians at VRCC put Chase on maintenance medications and examine Chase every three months to be sure that the cancer hasn't returned. "They're very caring people," says Ms. Harrison. "Chase actually enjoys visiting them."

Ms. Harrison is delighted with the care Chase received. Chase, now at thirteen years old, is more energetic than he had been before the cancer. "I hope that people realize that there are options when dealing with cancer. We were lucky, but we had several good options. We went from a grim diagnosis to a great outcome."

DOES MY PET HAVE CANCER?

It's important that your veterinarian examine your pet as soon as possible to determine if the symptoms are caused by cancer. Fifty percent of all cancers are completely curable, so don't delay. Common symptoms that should warn you to take your pet to a veterinarian include the following (50):

- Lack of appetite
- Vomiting
- Lethargy

- Weakness
- Weight loss
- Unexplained excessive thirst
- Increased urination
- Blood in urine or feces
- Bleeding or unusual discharge from any orifice
- Unusual lumps or bumps
- Sores that don't heal
- Lameness or stiffness that won't go away
- Strong, repulsive odor
- Difficulty breathing or swallowing
- Difficulty eating
- Inability to enjoy normally pleasant activities (walks with a dog or playing chase the feather with a cat)
- Difficulty urinating or defecating
- Seizures in an older pet who has not had seizures previously

Not all of these symptoms mean that your pet has cancer, but they can be serious enough to make you seek veterinary attention if your pet has any of them.

WHAT IS CANCER?

Let's consider what cancer really is. In cancer, cells mutate and grow abnormally, often destroying the "good" cells in preference to their pattern. Cancer isn't just one disease, but several. Some cancers attack the skin; others attack the blood. Still others attack bones, connective tissue, or organs. Any organ or system in a dog or cat can harbor cancer. Some cancers are curable; some are not at this time. In most cases, veterinary medicine can do something to treat or combat cancer.

It's helpful to understand certain terminology when dealing with cancer. Let's look at some words and their meanings.

Tumor

A common term used to describe cancer is *tumor*, but not all cancers are tumors and not all tumors are cancerous. A tumor is, by definition, a swollen area. On a dog or cat, a tumor is a self-contained growth arising from existing tissue that grows independent of the existing tissue and has no physiological function. A tumor may be malignant or benign; it may be nothing to worry about, or it may be something serious.

Neoplasia (neoplasm, singular)

A word you may hear from your veterinarian is *neoplasia* or *neoplasm*. It's an abnormal new growth of tissue or a tumor. Like the word "tumor," "neoplasm" doesn't define whether the growth is malignant or benign.

Malignant versus Benign

Malignant and *benign* are two descriptions of how a tumor may act. A benign tumor or neoplasm is localized, meaning that it is in only one place. It's non-infiltrative—it won't spread past the tissue it is in. Benign tumors usually can be removed without too much difficulty.

However, just because the tumor is benign doesn't mean it can't cause problems. Benign tumors can cause problems depending where they appear, such as in one of the organs.

Malignant tumors are the opposite of benign tumors. They are infiltrative, meaning that they can spread, and they will metastasize (spread to other parts of the body) if not caught quickly.

A third type of tumor is of intermediate malignancy. It will spread locally but will not metastasize.

TERMS TO KNOW

Adenoma—A tumor, usually benign, that appears on the skin

Benign—Used to describe a tumor that will not spread and is non-invasive

Cancer—Cells that mutate and grow abnormally

Chemotherapy—Treatment with medications; usually used for cancers that spread throughout the body.

Invasive—Used to describe a cancer that spreads into other organs or tissues

Malignant—Used to describe a tumor that will spread

Metastasize—The spread of cancer from a localized area to another site in the body

Oncologist—A doctor who specializes in the treatment of cancer.

Radiation therapy—Treatment of cancer using radiation at a particular site; usually used with cancers and tumors that are localized

Sarcoma—A malignant type of tumor

Surgery—Removal of a tumor or cancer; usually used with cancers and tumors that are localized.

Tumor—A growth

Sarcomas, Adenomas, and Carcinomas

You may hear the words *sarcoma* or *adenoma* being used at some point. *Sarcomas* are a type of malignant tumor that comes from connective tissues within the body (not on the skin). These tumors are frequently found beneath the skin itself.

Adenomas are tumors; they are usually benign or have a low malignancy when they appear on the skin. These are usually glandular in origin.

Carcinomas are malignant tumors arising from epithelial cells—skin cells and cells that line or cover different organs.

WHAT CAUSES CANCER?

Now that you know that cancer isn't one particular disease, but a host of diseases, you can understand that cancer doesn't have one cause. Some of the causes of cancer include the following:

- Environmental substances
- Rancid food (54)
- Age
- Heredity or congenital factors
- Vaccinations
- Trauma
- Viruses
- Other unknown causes (idiopathic)

Not all of these things may cause cancer in pets. For example, cats are particularly susceptible to vaccination-site tumors; dogs are not. Some tumors and cancers occur in intact dogs and cats, whereas a pet who is spayed or neutered has little or no chance of having the same types of cancers. However, spaying or neutering your pet doesn't guarantee your pet won't develop cancer. Maggie's first dog, Conan, developed prostate cancer even though he had been neutered at a very early age. At the same time, many intact dogs never develop anal tumors or prostate cancer, so there's no guarantee.

CAN CANCER BE SUCCESSFULLY TREATED?

If you've picked up this book, you're probably looking for the answer to that very question. The answer is complicated, because some cancers are curable, some can be treated as chronic conditions, and others may not have many treatments available. However, most oncologists can or will tell you that they can do *something* when it comes to treating cancer.

Much of the success in treating cancer comes from early diagnosis. Many cancers in their earliest stages are treatable, if not curable. In later stages, treatment becomes trickier and more costly, but there's usually something you can do, at least to make your pet comfortable.

In this book, we present several case studies, some about successful treatments and others unsuccessful. When considering whether to treat cancer, remember that cancer research has made cancer treatment of even five years ago look archaic by comparison. Don't let people's stories of ten or even a few years ago convince you that you shouldn't treat your pet's cancer. Get the facts from your veterinarian and veterinary oncologist first. They should be the people you trust to give you good answers when considering whether you should treat your pet or not.

CANCER STATISTICS IN DOGS AND CATS

- ➤ Cancer is the leading cause of death in dogs and cats over ten years old.
- ➤ Forty-seven percent of dogs and 32 percent of cats over ten years old die of cancer.
- ➤ Average lifespan of a dog treated for lymphoma is fifteen months.
- ➤ Over eight thousand dogs are affected by osteosarcoma each year.
- ➤ Eighty percent of dogs with advanced oral and digital melanoma die within eight to ten months of treatment.
- ➤ Hemangiosarcoma accounts for 5 percent of all non-skin malignancies in dogs.

- Approximately 450 out of 100,000 dogs will develop some sort of skin cancer over their lifetimes.
- Twenty to 30 percent of all canine skin tumors are malignant.
- About 12 percent of all canine skin growths are histiocytomas (a benign tumor).
- Perianal growths are the third most common growths in dogs, and 91 percent are benign.
- Fifty percent of breast cancers are malignant. Approximately two out of every one thousand female dogs will develop mammary cancer, with most cases being found in dogs ten to eleven years of age.
- Lymphoma affects 84 in 100,000 dogs over ten years old.
- Twenty-five percent of all cat cancers are skin cancers; 50 to 65 percent are malignant.
- Mammary cancer accounts for 17 percent of all tumors in cats. Approximately 25 female cats out of 100,000 get mammary tumors.
- Two hundred out of 100,000 cats will get feline lymphoma.
- Squamous cell cancers make up 9 to 25 percent of all feline skin cancers.
- One third of all feline tumors are some form of feline lymphoma.
- Cats who are feline leukemia (FELV) positive are sixty times more likely to get feline lymphoma than cats who are FELV negative.
- Seventy percent of all cat with feline lymphoma are FELV positive.
- One in one thousand to one in ten thousand cats are affected by vaccine-associated sarcomas.
- Ten percent of all feline cancer occurs in the mouth.
- Sixty to seventy percent of all oral cancer is squamous cell carcinoma.

FACT AND FICTION SURROUNDING CANCER

There are many fallacies concerning cancer. In this chapter we hope to dispel some of the myths surrounding this disease.

- **Cancer is a death sentence.** FALSE. Cancer is the most treatable of the chronic diseases. While many cancers are indeed fatal, through current techniques, treatments put many cancers into remission or may give you several months to years of quality time with your pet.

- **It's better to wait and see if that lump is cancer.** FALSE. The sooner you have the cancer diagnosed, the sooner you can begin treatment.

- **Feeding a raw diet will prevent cancer.** FALSE. While feeding a balanced diet and diets specifically made to combat cancer will help prevent or fight cancer, feeding raw diets can be just as dangerous if your dog or cat eats a nutritionally imbalanced diet or if the food is spoiled (which may actually *cause* cancer).

- **Don't put your pet through radiation/chemotherapy. It will make your pet sick.** MOSTLY FALSE. Most pets tolerate chemotherapy and radiation well because veterinary oncologists have refined techniques for treating cancer. New medications for chemotherapy are constantly being developed that work at killing the cancer and not the good cells. Some pets still do have reactions, but those are becoming a thing of the past. Most reactions can be handled by premedicating, switching to other drugs, or lowering the dosages.

- **Cancer therapy is expensive.** DEPENDS. Removing tumors that haven't metastasized is very inexpensive, costing just the price of surgery and lab tests. Other cancers may cost thousands of dollars to treat but are still much less than treating a human with the same treatment. Even if treatment is expensive, you might be able to put your pet in a study for a lower cost alternative.

➤ **Preservatives in pet food cause cancer.** MOSTLY FALSE. The amount of preservatives in pet foods is so small that they are unlikely to affect your pet. Most of the preservatives are anti-oxidants intended to prevent rancidity. Rancid fat can contribute to cancer if your pet is constantly consuming it. However, preservatives in huge doses (doses thousands of times the amount in pet foods) can be toxic.

➤ **Holistic medicine should be tried instead of conventional medicine when dealing with cancer.** FALSE. Alternative or complementary medicine should be used in conjunction with conventional veterinary medicine to treat cancer and only under the supervision of your veterinarian and veterinary oncologist. Using alternative medicine instead of conventional medicine puts your pet at risk.

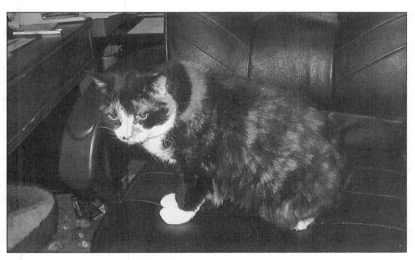

Not all older pets will develop cancer.
Samantha is 21 years old and cancer free.

OWNERS AND VET—A PARTNER FOR YOUR PET

You and your veterinarian should work together as partners for the health of your pet(s). As your pet's human advocate, you need to be informed and involved.

More than anyone else, a caring owner KNOWS her pet. You know your pet's regular routine, his habits and foibles, and what his normal behavior and health status are. As a veterinarian, Deb relies on the human half of the client/patient team in her exam room to help her do the best possible job of caring for the pet involved.

How can you do this? First, be observant. Pay attention to how your dog or cat acts when he feels good. Watch his normal appetite and elimination patterns. Keep track of how much he drinks on a normal day. Pay attention to his movement and how easily he gets up and down and how easily he jumps.

If your pet has a problem or a chronic ailment, keep a written record of your observations. This could be as detailed as a description of the stools or as simple as a note on the calendar when your pet has a seizure. If allergies suddenly start up, try to remember any changes in the environment—not just diet, but also rug cleaners, sprays used in the house, and so on. These bits of information are clues to help us in the hunt for the correct diagnosis.

Don't trust your memory—write it down! The more information you can provide, the easier it is to diagnose a problem. And the faster and more easily your vet can diagnose a problem, the faster she can treat your pet and get him back to normal.

We strongly encourage people to do a once-weekly home exam of their pets. Start with the nose and work backward. You can check eyes for discharge or changes, ears for any smell or discharge, the mouth for any growths or bad teeth. Dogs and cats have two of most things, so you have the chance to compare. If one ear is bright red and has a brown discharge and the other ear is a pale pink you know one ear has a problem! (As an aside here, Deb considers eye problems emergencies—flush the eye/s with artificial tears if you note a problem and call your veterinarian!)

Massage your dog's body gently, comparing the sides for symmetry and feeling for any lumps or bumps. Your pet will love this extra attention and you can pick up growths while they are very small. Gentle rubbing under even a relatively short coat like that of a Golden Retriever or a domestic shorthaired cat can still reveal many things. Check legs for muscle mass—the two legs should be approximately equal. If one leg is atrophied, you know there is a problem.

If your pet is vomiting or develops diarrhea—save a sample before you do a thorough cleanup. Diagnosing the cause of diarrhea without a fecal sample in the pet who is totally empty (the vet can't even get a sample doing a rectal exam) can be very frustrating.

When you do go to the veterinarian's office, bring a list of questions and concerns. If your vet is impatient or abrupt, maybe you need a different veterinarian. (Forgive them if they have a large number of emergencies that day, but only then!) Help your veterinarian by being clear and precise in your observations. It can be very frustrating when two people come in with the dog and one says the dog is having bloody diarrhea while the other person says no blood and really only slightly soft stool, not diarrhea at all! And we all know that the person who accompanies the dog to the vet is NEVER the person who feeds the dog junk food or overfeeds the dog in any way.

Respect your veterinarian if she says "I don't know" in answer to a question. She will research the problem and get back to you. This is much better than giving you false information. If your breed has some breed-specific problems or your dog or cat has some unusual health problems, don't hesitate to do some research on your own and take the information to your veterinarian. Your vet is caring for many dogs and cats of many breeds (and usually other species as well). Not every vet may read the Golden Retriever national newsletter and know about the new, unique problem showing up in Goldens.

SUMMARY

- Fifty percent of all cancer is curable.
- Cancer is the abnormal growth of cells.
- Cancer has a variety of causes but it is often a result of environment and hereditary factors.
- Learn the warning signs of cancer and seek veterinary attention if your pet has them.
- Learn to examine your pet. The more information you have to give your vet, the more likely your vet will arrive at a good diagnosis.
- Find out the available options for treatment of cancer. Techniques now are better than treatments even five years ago.

2

Common Canine Cancers

IN THIS CHAPTER
- Learn what cancers are common in dogs.
- Learn which skin tumors are benign and which are cancerous.
- Learn how to prevent certain common cancers such as breast cancer and testicular cancer.
- Learn why lymphoma is sometimes called a "good" cancer.

Case Study

Wiley, Deb's Belgian Tervuren, was just about seven-and-a-half years old when she found a lump on his rib cage. The bulge on his right side was not painful, but definitely not normal. Radiographs (x-rays) showed an aggressive mass invading the ribs and probably spreading to his lungs.

Deb knew that many difficult decisions lay ahead of her. Wiley was otherwise a young, healthy dog; many Belgian Tervurens compete actively in performance events like agility and obedience even after twelve years of age. She decided to pursue treatment, knowing that the prognosis was not good but feeling that any extra time, as long as Wiley was feeling good, was worth it.

Surgery to remove part of Wiley's rib cage, along with a biopsy, revealed a very aggressive case of hemangiosarcoma. She had his surgery done at the

Wiley a week before he died. Note the dark pigment
on front legs due to chemotherapy

*Cornell veterinary college, and she also consulted experts in chemotherapy
from Ohio State's veterinary college. Wiley bounced right back from his
surgery and went on to chemotherapy. He never missed a meal, and his
hair did not fall out as often happens with people.*

*For almost four months, Wiley did well. Then Deb noticed his feet oc-
casionally scuffing and a stumble here and there. One night almost four
months after his diagnosis, Wiley woke Deb up at 4 A.M. He went out to
urinate, ate a biscuit, then asked her to throw his tennis ball a few times.
They came back into the house, and Wiley went into nonstop seizures. Deb
knew she had lost the battle, and he was euthanized.*

We always second-guess ourselves. Should she have put him through surgery? Maybe not, but he healed rapidly and was chasing his ball within five days post-op. Should she have tried chemotherapy? Some dogs live for a year after surgery and chemo. Wiley gained only a few months, but he felt good and seemed to be enjoying life. Would she have put a twelve- or thirteen-year-old dog through the same plan? Deb doesn't know. These are critical decisions that are extremely personal, with no easy answers. That is what cancer deals us.

CANINE SKIN TUMORS[1]

Skin tumors account for about one third of all the canine tumors. Approximately 450 out of 100,000 dogs will develop some sort of skin cancer over their lifetimes (1). Mast cells are the most common, but **perianal** adenomas and lipomas are common as well.

Twenty to 30 percent of all canine skin tumors are malignant (1). Malignant cancers often grow rapidly and are fixed in place (not movable in the skin); they may be ulcerated on the surface. In contrast, benign tumors are usually slow growing, painless, movable in the skin and clearly circumscribed (have obvious borders). The location of the growth may be significant—for example, melanomas in the mouth tend to be more malignant than melanomas in the skin.

Just as in people, skin cancers in dogs may be influenced by the sun—for example, **squamous** cell cancers. Growths may also be associated with viruses such as the papillomas or warts and also with vaccine components (1). Genetic susceptibility may play a part in the development of many of these cancers. Skin growths are most commonly seen in older dogs, with a couple of exceptions, including viral papillomas and histiocytomas.

Diagnosing skin cancers may involve a variety of tests. A history

1. See also "Mast Cell Tumors" in chapter 4.

of the growth is important—how fast it grew, any exposures your pet might have had, and so on. A careful physical exam gives your veterinarian an idea of your dog's overall health and may reveal other smaller growths.

Cytology, checking a few cells from the surface of the growth or aspirating some cells with a needle, may be all that is needed to get a diagnosis. More commonly, a biopsy, where the growth or at least a piece of the growth is removed for microscopic study, is needed. Great care is taken not to disturb the cells on the surface of the sample. A biopsy may actually be curative in that the entire growth may be removed; it may be reductive in that the growth is reduced in size so that additional therapy such as radiation will be more successful; or it may be palliative, reducing any discomfort your dog has. A biopsy may be necessary to differentiate a benign cyst from a true cancer.

Added therapies may be required to completely treat your dog's skin cancer. **Cryosurgery,** radiation, **hyperthermy,** and additional surgery may all be part of your dog's treatment plan. Chemotherapy is rarely helpful for skin tumors.

Common skin cancers include papillomas, histiocytomas, lipomas, and perianal growths.

Papillomas

Papillomas are best known as "warts." Just as in people, most of these tumors are associated with viruses that stimulate the extra cell growth. Multiple small growths are common on young dogs. The head, feet, and mouth areas are the most likely locations.

Papillomas tend to be raised, rough surfaced, light colored, and hairless. They are not usually ulcerated unless they get rubbed or scratched heavily.

The DNA for these viruses is species specific, so they are *not* contagious to people (and vice versa—you won't spread your warts to

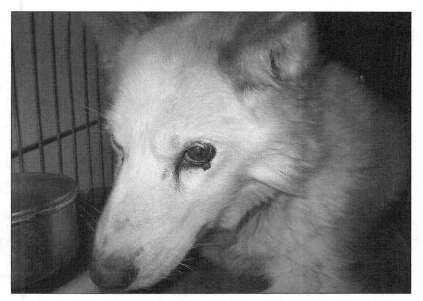

The papillomas on Lights shown here are benign tumors.

your dog!) These warts are contagious from dog to dog but require close contact. In general, these benign growths resolve on their own in young dogs (1).

Older dogs may just have solitary growths; they can appear on the head, feet, or eyelids. These are not usually associated with viruses but are seen in breeds such as cocker spaniels and Kerry blue terriers (1).

Histiocytomas

Histiocytomas are benign young-dog skin growths. About 12 percent of all canine skin growths are histiocytomas (1). These growths are almost always single and appear like raised, slightly red, round buttons. The ears, legs, and face are common sites.

Histiocytomas usually appear at somewhere around one to two

years of age in dogs and disappear in about three months. These growths almost always regress (disappear) on their own, but sometimes they are removed surgically. Deb's Lab had a histiocytoma on her cheek when she was young.

Breeds with a higher incidence of histiocytomas include Boxers, Cocker Spaniels, Great Danes, Doberman Pinschers, Dachshunds, Scottish Terriers, Labrador Retrievers, Shetland Sheepdogs, Rottweilers, and Miniature Schnauzers (1, 2).

Perianal Growths

Perianal growths are most common in male dogs and are considered the third most common tumor overall in dogs (1). Ninety-one percent of these tumors are benign. Older, intact (un-neutered) males are the most likely to have perianal adenomas.

These growths appear around the rectum on the hairless skin. If they grow too large, they may outstrip their blood supply and will ulcerate. It is suspected that these growths are **androgen** dependent. They may appear in association with testicular interstitital tumors. Neutering and/or surgery to remove the growths is usually curative. Breeds with a predisposition to benign perianal adenomas are Cocker Spaniels, Beagles, Bulldogs, Samoyeds, Shih Tzus, and Lhasa Apsos (1,2).

Rarely, these growths are malignant adenocarcinomas. The tumors are not hormone dependent and require extensive surgery with follow-up radiation and/or chemotherapy. Siberian Huskies as a breed are predisposed to the malignant form (2).

Anal sac adenocarcinomas are often confused with perianal adenomas because of their location. These malignant tumors are seen most often in the anal glands (small glands on either side of the rectum) of female dogs. They frequently have metastasized before diagnosis and may cause a cancer-associated increase in calcium—**malignancy hypercalcemia**.

Lipomas

Lipomas, or fatty tumors, are just that—cancers made up of fat cells. These growths are round, soft to the touch, and usually easy to move. They have obvious margins and may be solitary or multiple. Many of the "lumps" we feel on our older dogs are lipomas.

These tumors are almost always benign though there is a rare malignant version. While people mistakenly assume that these lumps are associated with overweight dogs, even trim dogs can develop lipomas. Your veterinarian may do a fine needle aspirate to check out some cells to be sure the growth is just a lipoma. The aspirate will often look "greasy" right on the slide.

Surgery may be done simply to make your dog more comfortable, especially if the lipoma is quite large and might interfere with your dog's movement. These growths often occur along your dog's body— the ribcage and abdominal areas. Surgery is curative.

Middle-aged female dogs are the most common victims of this type of cancer. Breeds that show a predisposition to lipomas include Doberman Pinschers, Labrador Retrievers, Miniature Schnauzers, Cocker Spaniels, Dachshunds, and Weimaraners. Even mixed-breed dogs may develop lipomas, though.

CANINE MAMMARY (BREAST) CANCER

As a group, mammary or breast cancers are the most common type of cancer in female dogs. About 50 percent of these cancers are **malignant**. Approximately two out of every one thousand female dogs will develop mammary cancer, with most cases being found in dogs ten to eleven years of age (1).

Breast cancer is usually first noticed as a small lump on your dog's belly when you rub it. Every small, firm lump should be checked by your veterinarian. She may want to do a **fine needle aspirate** (FNA) to look at the types of cells she finds. Your vet may decide to do a surgical **biopsy** (often the entire growth can be removed at that time).

Rarely, a dog has a widespread area of swollen, red, and inflamed mammary tissues. This could be **mastitis** (infection of the mammary glands) or **inflammatory carcinoma**—an aggressive and nasty cancer. Again, it is important to visit your veterinarian to evaluate the situation.

Signs You See

You may feel small, firm lumps along the **mammary chain**, often associated with nipples. You might also see swollen, red, inflamed tissue along the mammary chain.

Diagnosis

Diagnosis is usually done via an FNA—remember, this gives you a definite answer if cancer cells show up; if it is negative, it could simply mean that the needle missed all the cancer cells

A biopsy may be an alternative; it can even be curative for small, **benign** cancers. The primary types of mammary cancers seen in dogs are **adenomas** and **carcinomas.**

Treatment

Surgery is the best way to deal with mammary tumors in dogs. Ideally, your vet performs a wide surgical excision that leaves only normal tissue behind. Your vet should always send off tissue samples for microscopic examination. If cancer cells are found at the edges, your dog may need another surgery. Don't be dismayed at a long incision—incisions heal from side to side, not end to end!

For a benign cancer, total surgical removal can be curative.

Currently, it is not felt that spaying a dog at the same time as removing the mammary tumors makes any difference in her prognosis. Benign mammary tumors tend to be hormone responsive, but most malignant ones aren't.

At the time of surgery, your veterinarian will take radiographs (x-rays) of her chest to check for lung **metastases** and possibly also of her back region to look for metastases to the **sublumbar** lymph nodes. Your vet may remove a **lymph node** to look for microscopic spread of the cancer cells.

Some dogs have more than one lump, and they can all be removed at the same time—again, with wide excisions.

Chemotherapy is not especially helpful for dogs with mammary cancer although veterinarians are looking at **doxirubicin** as a possibility. **Radiation** is not very useful either. **Tamoxifen** (a hormone-like substance) does not seem to help and can cause your female dog to have **vulvar** swelling, appear to be in heat, and in general cause more problems.

Prognosis

Mammary tumors are among the few canine tumors that have staging and grading evaluations. These evaluations do influence prognosis. Grades range from 0—a small, limited growth with no spread beyond the surgical margins, to III, which has metastases beyond the localized region (e.g., to the lungs, usually). Obviously you want your dog to be rated Grade 0. Staging considers three factors—the size of the tumor (with less than three centimeters being best) the presence or absence of lymph node infiltration, and whether or not there are distant metastases (again, most likely to the lungs). Dogs with small tumors, cleanly removed and with no metastases, have an 80 percent chance of still being alive two years after their initial surgery. Dogs with large tumors and metastases have only a 40 percent chance of living longer than two years. **Sarcomas** are an unusual type of mammary tumor in dogs, but as with inflammatory carcinomas they are very aggressive and have a poor prognosis, with most dogs dying within nine to twelve months (2).

The prognosis is not influenced by the dog's breed, age, whether or not she is spayed, or the number of tumors found.

Prevention and Care

Despite being common, mammary tumors are easy to prevent in dogs. If you **spay** your bitch before her first **estrus (heat or season)** she is at 0.5 percent risk of ever developing mammary tumors. After one to two heats, the risk goes up to 8 percent and after two heats the risk is at 26 percent and stays there.

Avoiding the use of **progestins** (primarily used to prevent unwanted pregnancies due to "mistake breedings") is helpful. While using these drugs stimulates benign mammary tumors, you would prefer that your bitch didn't get any at all!

It has been shown that if your bitch is fit and trim between nine and twelve months of age, she will have a lower incidence of mammary tumors. We know that fitness is important for many reasons, especially in young, growing dogs—here is one more good reason to keep your puppies lean.

Dogs who have been treated for mammary tumors do best on a low-fat, but reasonably high-protein, diet.

Breed Predispositions

Breeds with a higher incidence of mammary tumors include Poodles, Brittanys, English Setters, Pointers, Boston Terriers, Fox Terriers, and Cocker Spaniels. Breeds with a low incidence of mammary tumors include Boxers, Greyhounds, Beagles, and Chihuahuas (2).

CANINE LYMPHOMA

If it is possible to speak of such a thing as "good" cancer, then *lymphoma* often fits the bill. While true cures are rare, many dogs diagnosed with lymphoma do quite well for long periods of time under treatment. This is a type of cancer that can and does strike both the young and the old. Risk for dogs older than ten is 84 out of 100,000 with six- to nine-year-old dogs being the primary victims (1). Lymphomas comprise 7 to 24 percent of all canine neoplasias.

Lymphomas come in many different forms. About 80 percent of all lymphomas are **multicentric**—lymph nodes in many areas of the body are affected. Approximately 7 percent are **alimentary,** meaning the tumors stick to the digestive tract, such as the intestines. Other areas are the **cranial mediastinum** (the area inside the chest, right in front of the heart where there is lymphatic tissue); in the skin; and even in the brain, spinal cord, or eye. In fact, ocular or eye lymphoma is the second most common eye tumor in both dogs and cats (2).

Lymphomas also vary in exactly which type of lymphoid cell is involved—T or B. While both types of cells normally fight infection, they do work in different ways. That means cancers of those cells may act differently as well.

Signs You Can See

Most owners first notice swollen lymph nodes on a pet that may still be acting just fine. The lymph nodes of the **prescapular** area (in front of the shoulder) and **submandibular** area (under the jaw) are often the first lymph nodes to swell and be noticed. While the swelling may be dramatic, these swollen glands are usually painless. If the swelling alone doesn't send you rushing off to your veterinarian, eventually Fido's illness will. About 40 percent of dogs with lymphoma show weight loss, lethargy, and loss of appetite. If they have the alimentary or intestinal form, dogs may vomit and have diarrhea. Dogs with ocular or **central nervous system** signs will have vision problems, lack of coordination, or behavior changes.

Dogs with **cutaneous** or skin forms of lymphoma may show very nonspecific skin problems—redness, dandruff, hair loss, and so on.

Dogs with lymphoma often get **paraneoplastic syndromes,** or changes in body functions that are related to the cancer. With lymphoma, one of the common changes is an increase in calcium in the blood, or **hypercalcemia.** This problem is most often seen with T-cell type lymphomas. Increased calcium can have many different effects. Most dogs drink more, may develop kidney problems, and eventually can have heart problems, especially arrhythmias where the heart beats erratically.

Anemia, possibly with related weakness, is seen in 38 percent of dogs with lymphomas.

Diagnosis

It sounds like diagnosing lymphoma should be easy. You simply check your dog's lymph nodes for swelling. It is not quite that simple, however. Lymph nodes can swell whenever they are working hard at fighting infections. That includes bacteria, parasites, viruses, and even some fungal infections. As always, a pet with suspected cancer should have a **minimum data base (MDB)** done. This includes a complete blood count (CBC) to check for anemia and to make sure your dog has plenty of platelets to help with blood clotting; a full panel to look for liver or kidney problems and also to check calcium levels in the blood; a urinalysis to look for kidney problems; and usually a chest radiograph (X ray). Some veterinarians may want a bone marrow sample to see if your dog is still producing red and white blood cells normally.

Ultrasound can be useful both for diagnosis and staging (determining if your pet has metastases, for example).

With the different types of lymphoma, your dog may show vomiting and diarrhea, so the vet should do a fecal check, radiographs (x-rays) of the abdomen, and possibly even a dye study of the intestines. It may be difficult to differentiate between inflammatory bowel disease and early stages of alimentary lymphoma (19). This can be particularly important in dogs like Basenjis who have a known predilection for an immune intestinal problem.

A special eye exam or dye study of the spinal cord may be indicated if your dog shows vision or **neurologic** signs.

Often a fine needle aspirate sample is taken from a swollen lymph node, or an entire lymph node may be removed for biopsy. Luckily, many lymph nodes are near the surface of the body and fairly easy to remove. With a lymph node removed, not only will you find out if cancer is present or not, but you can grade the tumor. The pathologist will look for **telomerase** activity (an evaluation of **mitosis**—looking at how fast the cells are reproducing and if they reproduce in a normal manner). Additionally, the lymphoid cells can be checked to see if they are B or T cells.

B-cell lymphomas tend to have a better prognosis and less hypercalcemia than T-cell tumors. Tumors with a high grade (very blastic, immature cells) are more responsive to chemotherapy, so that is also a good sign.

Treatment

With no treatment, most dogs will die in four to six weeks after diagnosis and will be ill for much of that time. Using prednisolone alone may give a dog two to three months of decent-quality life.

Lymphomas are classically treated with **chemotherapy**. Remember that in dogs we see fewer side effects than in humans, since dogs are treated less aggressively. We know that no matter what, our dogs have no chance of living much beyond another five to ten years, so we treat to put them in **remission** and keep them comfortable. Lymphomas in dogs are considered to be the cancers most responsive to chemotherapy (19).

Single chemotherapy drugs such as doxorubicin may add six to twelve good months to your dog's life. Combination protocols (mixes of different chemotherapy drugs in a carefully planned dosage schedule can keep dogs cancer free for up to three years (1). It is amazing to see the rapid response to any type of treatment for lymphoma. Literally, within days or even hours, the glands shrink and the dogs feel much better. Current response rates to initial chemotherapy are 80 to 90 percent responding, with survival times of 250 to 300 days not unusual (19).

The treatment goal is to get a remission and then keep it for as long as possible. Using prednisolone alone first may interfere with later treatment effectiveness, but it is included in many of the chemotherapy protocols. Ideally, the first remission lasts for six to twelve months. Some veterinarians recommend treating for at least two chemotherapy cycles after the cancer appears to be gone (2). Others stop therapy after a remission is achieved.

Combination protocols require careful planning. Drugs must be administered on the correct schedule; different drugs work differently; and overlapping toxicities must be avoided. Commonly used drugs include cyclophosphamide, which may cause sterile bloody urine; L-asparaginase, which is relatively mild in its effects on the marrow; actinomycin, which is actually an antibiotic with anti-tumor actions; doxorubicin, mentioned earlier; and lomustine (CCNU), which is good for cases with drug resistance but can be damaging to marrow.

Induction protocols use high levels of very strong drugs to knock the cancer down dramatically right at the start. This minimizes the chances of cells developing drug resistance. A **maintenance** protocol may use different drugs, lower dosages, or less frequent treatments.

Sadly, most lymphomas return at some point. If it has been a long time since your dog's last treatment, the vet might try using the same drugs again. However, cancer cells may develop drug resistance just as bacteria do to antibiotics. Some cells actually develop a kind of pump that pushes chemotherapy drugs out of them.

Chemotherapy effectiveness is enhanced by acting aggressively right from the start. Using the maximum dose, frequently and over a long period of time, is better than tiptoeing around with a low dose. Most immune stimulants have not been shown to help, but **autologous vaccines** may help, as may removing the **spleen**.

Side effects of the chemotherapy drugs may include inability to eat, vomiting, diarrhea, hair loss, and weakness. Heart difficulties can also be a side effect. Internally, the cells that fight infection may get wiped out along with blood cells. Frequent monitoring of blood counts is important and may even determine whether a treatment can be done on a given day.

When a lymphoma returns, veterinarians often go to "rescue protocols." These are chemotherapy protocols that may use different, perhaps more toxic drugs, to try and gain a remission again.

Unfortunately, immune therapy (such as using vaccines made from your dog's own cancer cells) has not proven to be very effective at this time.

Prognosis

The prognosis can vary greatly in lymphomas. Dogs with B-cell lymphomas tend to do better than dogs with T-cell lymphomas. Deb's parents' dog Ranger had an aggressive T-cell lymphoma, and he lived four months (though they did not do highly aggressive chemotherapy). Another dog Deb has known, Little Lala, had three very good years after her lymphoma diagnosis. As always, the overall health and age of your dog at the time of diagnosis is important. Still, 60 to 90 percent of the dogs with lymphoma live six months to a year after diagnosis and treatment (1). Considering the old adage about one human year equaling seven dog years, that isn't bad at all!

The response to the first set of treatments can be an important indicator of prognosis. Dogs who respond with a long remission are more likely to respond again to "rescue" therapy.

Spayed females seem to do better, and dogs who do not have hypercalcemia have better survival times (19). Most dogs do better if they do not receive steroids before a definitive chemotherapy protocol (19). There are molecular markers that are predictive of survival times, but these are not commercially available yet. These include AgNOR and Ki-67 (19). Dogs with mediastinal lymphoma do not generally do well.

Prevention and Care

Certainly, lymphomas tend to appear in pets with weak immune systems. Keeping your dog as healthy as possible can't hurt and might help. As with any cancer, early detection and treatment increases the odds for success. Lymphomas do show up in pets with genetic problems such as chromosome errors (often not easy to detect without special lab techniques).

There have been suggestions of a retrovirus associated with lymphomas (2), but this has not been conclusively determined. There are also questions about exposures to magnetic fields (2). Exposure to some herbicides, especially 2-4D or 2-4 dichloro phenoxyacetic acid, is associated with chromosome changes and an increased risk of lymphoma (1). Merely living in an area with industrial toxins may put your pet (and possibly you) at a higher risk for lymphoma (19).

Breed Predispositions

An increased risk of developing lymphoma has been noted in a wide variety of dog breeds (1, 2). Boxers, Bassett Hounds, Airedales, Bulldogs, Scottish Terriers, and St. Bernards are on many lists. German Shepherds, Poodles, Beagles, and Golden Retrievers also seem predisposed. At Deb's clinic, Deb feels that she sees mostly Golden Retrievers with lymphomas, but that may be skewed because she sees so many Goldens to begin with! Certainly, lines or families of Bullmastiffs, Otterhounds (19), and Rottweilers seem prone to lymphoma as well. Mixed breeds can certainly come down with lymphoma, as did Lala. Luckily, Dachshunds, Pomeranians, and Cocker Spaniels seem to have fewer lymphoma cases than would be expected!

Any dog with immune problems has an increased risk of cancer, with lymphoma near the top of the list (19).

CANINE HEMANGIOSARCOMA

Hemangiosarcoma is a devastating tumor in dogs. More hemangiosarcomas are found in dogs than in any other species (1). It ranks as the second most common type of cancer in dogs overall. For Deb, personally, it is the cancer that took her vital, active Belgian Tervuren Wiley at just eight years, one week, and one day of life. So she, of course, hates it with a vengeance. Wiley was typical in that this cancer seems to hit middle-aged dogs (eight to thirteen years of age) and perhaps males more than females.

Hemangiosarcoma is a tumor of blood vessels. It often grows in areas like the spleen, liver, and heart, which are very **vascular**. It is a fragile tumor and can rupture easily with trauma. When it does rupture, your dog may bleed extensively, even to the point of death.

Signs You Can See
The first indication of something wrong with your dog may simply be sudden and unexpected death. You may leave for work in the morning and come home to find your dog peacefully curled in his bed, dead. This happens when an internal tumor ruptures and your dog bleeds to death internally. Not painful for the dog, who experiences just increasing weakness, but certainly a painful shock for you!

Other dogs show weakness, often in cycles. In these cases, a small internal tumor may rupture, weakening your dog, but the rupture clots and your dog fights back. Rarely, you will notice a growth or distended abdomen indicating a tumor growing or fluid filling up the abdomen. On Wiley, Deb noticed an area on his rib cage that was a growth (once again, the importance of those weekly checks!)

Hemangiosarcoma also likes to grow on the right atrium of the heart. If a tumor there ruptures, your dog may show severe and sudden heart failure signs as the blood builds up in the sac around the heart, preventing it from pumping normally.

If your dog becomes weak fairly suddenly, has pale gums and perhaps labored breathing, head for your vet!

Diagnosis

Diagnosing hemangiosarcoma relies heavily on radiographs (x-rays) and ultrasounds—looking for unusual growths, swollen outlines of the right **atrium** of the heart, the spleen, or the liver. If it is growing in bones, such as Wiley's case in the rib, the bone may appear **lytic** or moth-eaten. Sometimes hemangiosarcoma will show up as a skin growth, but that is not nearly as common as the internal forms.

Your veterinarian will try to differentiate a **hematoma** (bruise leading to bleeding and a swollen appearance) of the spleen from a tumor in the spleen. This may actually require surgery and a biopsy to be certain.

Sometimes your pet will show abnormal red blood cells on blood work. Anemia, low numbers of **platelets,** and even *DIC* (**disseminated intravascular coagulation**—a problem with clotting so that your pet can't stop bleeding) are possible. Many, if not most, cases are diagnosed on autopsy after your dog suddenly and unexpectedly dies.

Treatment

Treating hemangiosarcoma is a challenge. If you are lucky and all your dog has is a small skin tumor, surgery might even be a cure. Sadly, most dogs have the internal form and by the time it is apparent, there has already been **metastasis**. It is estimated that in 70 to 80 percent of dogs with hemangiosarcoma, it has already have spread to the liver, lungs, and brain by the time of diagnosis (1).

Surgery to remove the spleen may help—if only by removing a source of possible heavy bleeding. In Wiley's case, the affected rib and the two ribs on either side were removed along with part of his chest wall. Sadly, he already had metastases to his lungs.

Following any surgeries, the next step is aggressive chemotherapy. Combination protocols are used most of the time and often include adriamycin (doxorubicin), which can have cumulative cardiac (heart) effects. Better protocols are being adopted all the time. Liposomal-muramyl tripeptide phosphatidylethanolamine (L-MTP-PE) is an immune therapy that may help. Wiley did go on chemotherapy and handled it very well—never missing a single meal!

Prognosis

The prognosis for cure (with the exception of skin hemangiosarcomas) is virtually zero. Most dogs die from either rupture of the primary tumor or metastases. Fewer than 10 percent live for a year. Dogs with pulmonary metastases tend to have an increased chance of brain metastases as well (2).

Wiley died four months after diagnosis. His cancer had spread to his brain and he suddenly started having seizures that would not stop early one morning. Deb had a clear sign that it was time to end the battle.

Prevention and Care

In people, exposures to arsenicals, vinyl chlorides, and thorium dioxide may be associated with a greater risk of developing hemangiosarcoma (1). Areas of the body that have had local irradiation (heavy irradiation as for cancer treatments, not diagnostic radiation) may have increased risk for skin hemangiosarcomas.

If your dog is diagnosed with hemangiosarcoma, you need to be as supportive as possible. Minimize chances of bruising or trauma. Decide whether it makes sense to try and treat your dog even though the prognosis is so poor—not always an easy decision. Deb went ahead with aggressive treatment for Wiley as he was an otherwise young and healthy dog. If he had been twelve years old, she might have elected hospice care.

Watch for signs of metastasis such as dragging paws or lack of coordination to indicate spread to the brain. And be prepared to accept sudden death.

Breed Predispostitions

Hemangiosarcoma has been seen in virtually all breeds, including mixed breeds. German Shepherds seem to have an increased incidence of internal hemangiosarcoma and, while we don't have the latest health survey results at this time, we suspect the Belgian breeds do as well. Whippets, Salukis, Bloodhounds, and English Pointers seem to be more likely to have cutaneous hemangiosarcoma (1).

CANINE BONE CANCER

The most common type of bone cancer in dogs is osteosarcoma— "osteo" meaning bone. Fully 80 percent of all primary canine bone tumors are osteosarcomas (2). Most of what we discuss here is from work on osteosarcomas. Great strides have been made in recent years in treating bone cancer in pets, especially dogs.

Signs You Can See

Most primary bone cancers occur in large breed dogs and in the **appendicular** or limb bones up to 75 percent of the time (1, 2). You might notice that your dog is lame in one leg, often with a fairly sudden onset. Certain areas on your dog's legs may be painful to the touch. Some dogs have swollen areas on their legs, possibly with redness and heat around the swollen area.

Front legs are twice as likely to be involved as rear legs in large breed dogs. The **distal radius** (far end of the bone between the elbow and the bend of the **carpus**), along with the **proximal humerus** (the bone between the shoulder blade and elbow, at the end closest to the shoulder blade) are the most common sites (1).

Small breed dogs (fifty pounds and under) are more likely to have bone cancer in **axial** bones—bones that are part of the main body, such as bones in the head (2). If they do get bone cancer in leg bones, it will tend to be in the rear legs. The **femur** (large bone from hip to knee or **stifle**) and **tibia** (bone from knee or stifle to **hock**) are the most common leg bone sites in small dogs (2).

Rarely, the first sign is a fracture or broken bone. A dog may simply be running in the yard when a leg breaks. This happens because the tumor destroys the normal bone, weakening the leg.

Diagnosis

Diagnosis usually involves a couple of different steps. **Radiographs**, or x-rays, are almost always taken. Your veterinarian looks for areas of bone destruction or new bone formation and checks to see if the changes cross over a joint. Bone cancers do not cross over joints, while infections of the bone might. There may be a great deal of soft tissue swelling around the cancerous areas as well.

A **bone scan** or an **MRI (magnetic resonance imaging)** are both useful tests, but they are not available at most veterinarians and are not usually necessary for a diagnosis. A small needle **biopsy** can have as close as 92 percent accuracy in diagnosing bone cancer as well.

Your veterinarian will also want to run a complete blood workup and do radiographs of your dog's chest. These radiographs are looking for **metastasis** or spread of the cancer into the lungs. Even if the lung radiographs appear normal, almost 90 percent of all dogs do already have spread of their cancer when they are diagnosed (the cancerous areas may just be too small to be detected).

Your veterinarian will be ruling out other problems such as **osteomyelitis** or bacterial infections of the bone, fungal infections of the bone, or cancer in the bones that is actually a metastasis of a different type of cancer (not primary bone cancer itself). In addition, you want to be sure that your dog is in reasonable health and able to withstand anesthesia and surgery, as most bone cancer treatment protocols involve at least some surgery.

Treatment

Amputation of the involved leg has been the standard first step in treating bone cancer. This remains part of the standard bone cancer treatment regimens today.

Techniques have been developed for **limb sparing** as well. In this surgery, the cancerous parts of the bone are removed and sterile bone from a donor dog is put in their place. This can be attempted only if the dog has just one leg with cancer and less than 50 percent of the bone is cancerous. The dog needs to be in good health otherwise, as this is a stressful surgery with great risk of infection. Most of these dogs have follow-up radiation or chemotherapy as well. Clearly, limb sparing is not being done at most veterinary clinics as a source of bone—that is, a bone bank—must be available. Limb sparing has not been shown to increase the survival time of the dogs with bone cancer, but it may make some of them more comfortable.

Many of the recent advances have come in the form of newer versions of chemotherapy. Cisplatin and carboplatin are both drugs that have been used for dogs with bone cancer. Cisplatin can be damaging to the kidneys, but when used with **MTP-PE (liposome encapsulated muramyl tripeptide phophatidylethanolamine)**, survival times can be lengthened. These medications should be used as early as possible (including pre-surgery) and can even be implanted near the cancer site. Chronic slow release methods such as **open cell polylactic acid**—polylactic acid plus a biodegradable polymer—may also add to survival time (1).

The use of chemotherapy seems to modify the spread of cancer to the lungs, but may not help at all with the spread to other bones. If the cancer shows up in the lungs, some studies recommend doing surgery to remove the lung lobes. There are caveats however—the primary bone tumor should be in remission, ideally for more than three hundred days. There should be only one to two nodules of cancer in the lungs, and a bone scan to look for cancer spread elsewhere should be clean (1).

Palliative radiation (using radiation to help alleviate pain) is becoming more widespread, and certainly managing the pain these dogs may suffer is an important part of their care. Injectable and/or oral pain medications may help immensely.

Sadly, most dogs die from metastatic spread to the lungs or from unrelieved pain.

Prognosis

The outcome for most bone cancer cases is not good long term. With surgery alone, owners can hope for three to five months. With chemotherapy added, some dogs survive eight months or more and of course, we all hope for the rare dog who beats the odds and is still alive and well over a year after treatment.

Bone cancers in dogs are staged similarly to human bone cancers. Grade I cancers have no sign of metastasis and a low reactive reading on their **histopathology**. Grade II cancers also have no obvious metastasis, but have a high reactive reading on histopathology. Grade III cancers already have signs of metastasis. Sadly, most dogs are diagnosed at Grade III (1).

As mentioned earlier, unremitting pain and metastasis, especially to the lungs, are usually the reasons for choosing euthanasia for dogs with osteosarcoma.

Prevention and Care

It is very difficult to prevent bone cancer in dogs. Certainly, choosing a small breed dog could lessen your chances of having a dog that develops bone cancer. Some bone cancers may develop secondary to earlier trauma, such as broken bones from being hit by a car. It is possible for a dog to develop bone cancer secondary to radiation treatment for another type of cancer, but that is quite rare (1).

Breed Predispositions

Large and giant breed dogs have the greatest risk of developing bone cancer over their lifetimes. The risk is felt to be about 150 times greater for large and giant breed dogs than for dogs under twenty pounds at adulthood (2).

The incidence peaks, with an early group of dogs at eighteen to twenty-four months and then most dogs at seven to nine years of age. While the young dog version is much less common, it tends to be very aggressive and those dogs have a very poor prognosis.

Breeds that seem to be over-represented include St. Bernards, Great Danes, Irish Setters, Doberman Pinschers, German Shepherds, and Golden Retrievers. Another subset of dogs will show bone cancer, but of the ribs, spine, and jaw rather than the more common leg form. These breeds are St. Bernards, Great Danes, and Rottweilers (1).

CANINE TESTICULAR CANCERS

Testicular cancers are not particularly common in male dogs, with the exception of **cryptorchids**. A cryptorchid dog is one who has one or more retained testicles—at least one testicle is still up inside the body instead of down in the scrotum where it belongs. You sometimes hear people misuse the word "monorchid" for those dogs with one testicle outside. Monorchid means the dog has only one testicle (whether inside or out), and that condition is quite rare in dogs. Up to 20 percent or more of all cryptorchid dogs develop some type of testicular cancer if the internal testicle is not surgically removed (27). It is felt that the higher temperatures the testicular tissues are exposed to inside the body are at least partially responsible for this.

So, dogs with crypotorchid testicles have a nine times higher risk of developing testicular cancer than a normal dog, and dogs with inguinal hernias have a four times greater risk (27). It should be clear that you would certainly want to neuter your cryptorchid dog!

There are three main types of testicular cancers. These are based on the types of cells they grow from—the Sertoli cell cancer, the seminoma, and the Leydig cell or interstitial cell cancer. They tend to be similar in many ways so we will discuss them as a group.

Signs You Can See

With some testicular cancers, you can feel an increase in your dog's testicle size. Still, particularly seminomas may not be palpable. And remember, if the affected testicle is retained inside the body, you may not notice anything at all until it gets quite large. Sometimes, people notice that the normal testicle is getting small and soft. This may be a secondary effect of an internal tumor that is secreting estrogen (one of the female hormones).

An internal tumor that is secreting estrogen can cause changes in coat—leading to hair loss or thinning. Some dogs may develop anemia from the effects of estrogen on the bone marrow. Other dogs may grow mammary tissue, attract male dogs, and show other signs of feminization—all side effects of estrogen production. About 25 percent of the dogs with Sertoli cell tumors show such feminization (27).

Diagnosis

There are a couple of ways a testicular cancer may be diagnosed. Certainly, feeling an external growth in the scrotum is the easiest (though your veterinarian will need to rule out infections, torsions, and other possible problems). If your dog suddenly starts showing signs of feminization and has a retained testicle, your veterinarian may do radiographs (x-rays) or ultrasound to look for a growth. Sometimes, blood tests checking for estrogen levels can be done as well. Rather than take a biopsy sample for diagnosis, most often the offending testicle(s) is totally removed and then looked at. This saves your dog from a second surgery.

Testicular cancers can show other secondary effects—such as prostate problems, hernias around the rectum, and tumors called perianal adenomas around the anus (2). If these problems show up in an intact dog, your veterinarian will check closely for any other evidence of testicular cancer.

Treatment

Treatment is quite straightforward—surgical removal of the cancerous testicle(s). Whether or not to leave a normal testicle is a decision you and your veterinarian need to make. Your dog may be sterile from the estrogen influence anyway, in which case there is certainly no reason to leave that one testicle. Leydig or interstitial cancers have a high rate of being bilateral (50 percent) so if this tumor is suspected, it makes sense to remove both testicles. Metastases are not common, but if they are found in the local lymph nodes or the lungs, radiation and/or chemotherapy may be started after surgery (2).

Prognosis

Luckily, most testicular cancers in dogs are slow-growing and fairly benign in that they aren't quick to metastasize. About 10 percent of these cancers will spread—usually first to local lymph nodes, then later to the lungs (27). Your veterinarian will check those two areas before doing any surgery and as part of the treatment plan for your pet.

Prevention and Care

A simple way to prevent testicular cancer is to remove the testicles by neutering or castrating your dog. Any dog with a retained testicle should have that testicle removed, even if you decide to leave the normal one. Obviously, it is better to remove that testicle before it is cancerous than to wait until cancer develops.

Military dogs who served in Southeast Asia had a higher than normal rate of seminomas. It is thought that exposure to pesticides and/or the chronic use of tetracycline to treat tick-borne diseases may be contributory factors.

Breed Predispositions

There have been no breed predispositions shown for testicular cancer in dogs.

ORAL CANCERS[2]

Oral cancers can be found in both dogs and cats. In dogs, the primary oral cancers are melanomas and fibrosarcomas. Cats tend to have squamous cell carcinomas (though dogs may get squamous cell carcinomas in their tonsils).

Signs You Can See

Pets with oral cancer (cancer in the mouth) may show a wide variety of signs. You might notice your pet drooling more than usual, and you may see a little blood in the drool. Your dog or cat may have terribly

---

2. See also Feline Oral Squamous Cell Carcinoma in chapter 4.

bad breath and show a sudden preference for soft food. Some pets will chew strangely (maybe just using one side of their jaw).

If your pet goes in for dentistry, your veterinarian may notice changes in the gums or an unusual set of loose teeth. It can be quite difficult to tell early oral cancers from dental disease! (16)

When you look into your pet's mouth, you might see a firm, pink mass off the top jaw. In a dog, this is likely to be a fibrosarcoma. A dark mass on the bottom jaw is more likely to be a melanoma.

The jawbones themselves are often involved in oral cancers, and the cancer may extend into the nasal passages. A pet may be brought in to check out a swelling on the jaw or nose or even a discharge from the nose.

Diagnosis

Oral Cancers may be diagnosed by radiographs (x-rays), biopsies, or fine needle aspirates. Often the growth will be noticed by the family or the veterinarian during a physical examination. An excisional biopsy (removing the entire growth) may be both diagnostic and curative.

Treatment

The treatment for oral cancers varies with the exact type of cancer. Radiation and surgery are the most common treatments, with chemotherapy being less successful. Some pets may even face the removal of a jaw bone. Still, pets adapt quite well to these types of surgeries.

Prognosis

The prognosis can vary a great deal with type of cancer. Dogs with squamous cell carcinoma of the tonsils often survive only four to six months after diagnosis (16).

Prevention and Care

These cancers are another testimony to the dangers of smoking. A study showed that cats who live with smokers for three to five years have a three to five times greater chance of developing oral or intestinal cancers! (16)

RETROPERITONEAL TUMORS IN DOGS

Retroperitoneal refers to the area near the kidneys (in your dog, picture the area of the abdomen right under the spine and right in front of the hind legs). This is an area that can be difficult to diagnose, as cancers can grow for quite a while before you notice any changes such as swelling or loss of appetite. The most common cancers of this area are sarcomas; they are generally aggressive and metastasize early (18). These sarcomas can include hemangiosarcomas and nonskeletal osteosarcomas.

Signs You Can See

You may notice that your pet is not eating well, that he is tired or weak, and that he is losing weight. A firm, swollen area may be detectable. Your pet may react to pain when touched in the abdominal area as well. Hind limb lameness may show up due to pressure on nerves (18).

Deb's little Lab, Gus, developed a rapidly growing mass that she could feel near the end of her rib cage. Her appetite was off a bit, but that was the only other sign. It is worth reminding you that doing at least weekly quick exams of your dog may catch cancers early and that feeding meals instead of leaving food down all the time will help you to notice changes like loss of appetite.

Diagnosis

Many different technologies may help to diagnose retroperitoneal cancers. Plain radiographs (x-rays), ultrasound, and CT scans may all pinpoint masses in this area. Rarely, a fine needle aspirate will pick up abnormal cells. Many cases are definitively diagnosed through exploratory surgery.

Treatment

Treatment for retroperitoneal tumors often starts with surgery. Your veterinary surgeon will attempt to remove as much as possible, if not all, of the cancerous growth. That may be difficult considering where the tumor is growing. **Intraoperative** radiation may be added to surgery in hopes of better results. Chemotherapy is sometimes tried but often the dogs dies either from local recurrence or metastatic problems before a full course of treatment can be given (18).

Prognosis

These are aggressive cancers with a poor prognosis for long-term survival. In Deb's dog, cancer was regrowing along her incision line by ten days after her surgery. From time of finding the mass until death, she had about a month of quality life. Not nearly enough!

SUMMARY

- One third of all dog tumors are skin tumors.
- Testicular cancer and mammary cancer can be prevented through spaying and neutering.
- Lymphoma is considered a "good cancer" because veterinarians can do something to treat it. Dogs who are treated for this cancer may add a year or more to their lives.

Some cancer, such as hemangiosarcoma, is very difficult to treat and has a poor prognosis. Other cancers, like bone cancer, can be treated with amputation and chemotherapy to give the dog up to eight months or more.

CHAPTER 3

Common Feline Cancers

IN THIS CHAPTER

- Learn which are the most common cancers that affect cats.
- Learn how to minimize your cat's risk of developing feline lymphoma by either vaccinating or preventing exposure to cats afflicted with feline-elevevated-leukemia virus (FELV) and feline immunodeficiency virus (FIV).
- Learn how to reduce your cat's chance of developing mammary tumors by spaying her.
- Learn how to identify vaccine-associated sarcomas and how to limit the chances of your cat developing them.

Some of the most common feline cancers are discussed here. Skin cancers are discussed as a group, with the other cancers described separately. We hope that this information will help you to make treatment and care decisions. Remember, while cats may seem to have the proverbial "nine lives," they still need our care, especially when faced with the challenge of a serious cancer.

Fang is proof that even older pets can do well with cancer therapy.

Case Study

Fang was a handsome seventeen-year-old black cat with beautiful eyes when Todd and Jane noticed he was losing some weight and vomiting more than normal. An occasional hairball was not unexpected, but this vomiting was more frequent.

Filled with concern for their elder statesman cat, they took Fang to their veterinarian. An ultrasound and radiographs (x-rays) showed some suspicious areas but nothing definitive. An exploratory surgery was the key to diagnosis—the biopsies showed that Fang had lymphoma.

At this point, Fang went off to see a local veterinarian with a specialty in oncology (cancer). Sadly, this veterinarian felt that Fang's cancer would not respond to any therapy and that his family should be happy they had enjoyed his company for so many years. He felt that Fang had only a few more months and they should simply make him comfortable.

This was not acceptable to Todd and Jane, so they contacted Cornell. Fang had the opportunity to sign on for a new experimental protocol but it would have involved travel to Cornell (two hours each way), and car rides were quite stressful for him. Finally, they worked out an arrangement with Fang's original veterinarian (who was surprised at the lengths Fang's family was willing to go to for him, but very supportive). A chemotherapy protocol was designed by the veterinarians at Cornell and the drugs administered locally to save Fang the road trips.

Obviously, in a seventeen-year-old cat, your goal is to get remission and keep him cancer free as long as possible, realizing that cure might not be realistic. Fang, however, has had other ideas.

Basically, Fang received one chemotherapy infusion every other week for twelve weeks. Since then he has had only an occasional prednisone tablet to help with some arthritis.

During his chemotherapy, Fang continued to lose weight, but he gained it all back later. And while he did lose a few patches of hair, they were small and his hair has all grown back. Fang also became a bit anemic, but that cleared when his treatments ended.

It has been two years now since Fang's cancer reared its head. He does have some signs of early kidney failure and gets subcutaneous fluids every other day at home. He is a bit slower and mellower but can still play and cuddle. Like any older cat, he sleeps more, especially in sunny spots. His attitude, appetite, and activity level are all very reasonable for a cat of his age.

Remember that Fang's original prognosis was for a few months at best. It took almost two months to get a complete and accurate diagnosis and get him started on treatments. Fang is certainly living proof that even older pets can benefit from cancer treatment!

Fang's owner Todd writes: "It is possible that Fang is one in a million, but even if the treatments had not been as effective, they were worth trying because cats tolerate chemotherapy very well without experiencing most of the side effects that people experience with chemotherapy. The chemotherapy injections were easy to administer and were quite inexpensive. Outside of the particulars of his treatment, we take things one day at a time. We know that Fang will have to leave us at some point, but for me, each day that he is with us is a gift."

At this writing, Fang remains a beloved member of his family—ruling over their Labrador Retrievers. He is living proof that cancers can be treated successfully even in senior-citizen pets and that dedicated owners working with a caring veterinarian can make treatment a reasonable option.

FELINE SKIN CANCERS

Skin cancers rank number two for feline cancers, right behind lymphoid tumors. They represent 25 percent of all cat cancers with 50 to 65 percent of them being malignant (1). Basal cell cancer gets the number one spot for cats, with 11 to 28 percent of all feline skin cancers (2). Mast cell tumors and squamous cell carcinomas or fibrosarcomas round out the top three.

Different factors can influence the development of skin cancers in cats. The sun and its ultraviolet radiation is implicated in many squamous cell cancers, especially in white cats. Viruses may stimulate cell changes and lead to cancers. **Hormone**s may play a role and vaccine components are associated with some fibrosarcomas. Genetics is also important, with some cat breeds showing predispositions to certain types of cancer.

Basal Cell Cancer

The term "basal cells" refers to cell layers in the skin. As mentioned, this is the most common type of skin cancer found in cats. Generally, it appears in cats that are seven to ten years of age. You might notice a round, movable growth in your cat's skin, usually a solitary lump and quite slow growing. Basal cell cancers tend to grow on the head. **Cytology** via a needle aspirate may be all that is needed for diagnosis, but many owners simply elect to go right for surgical removal. Most often, these are benign skin cancers and surgery is curative.

Siamese cats and domestic longhairs (think long-hair all-American kitty) are predisposed to basal cell cancers of the benign type (3).

Rarely, basal cell cancers take a malignant form. These growths fit most of the description above but tend to infiltrate into the tissues around them instead of being discrete little lumps. They do not often spread by metastasis but can be difficult to totally remove with surgery since they do infiltrate out. Surgery is again the treatment of choice, but radiation and/or chemotherapy may be needed as follow-up if the biopsy results show that some cancer cells may remain. Persian cats show in increased incidence of malignant basal cell tumors, so if you find a lump on your Persian's head, have it checked out right away.

Mast Cell Tumors

Mast cell tumors are another type of cancer that comes in many disguises. Mast cells are very reactive cells that take part in allergic reactions and cellular "clean-ups." These tumors can appear as solitary red, raised growths or red "plaquelike" areas. Most often they are found around the head or neck of your cat.

A careful **fine needle aspirate** for **cytology** may be sufficient for diagnosis, or you may elect a full biopsy. Your veterinarian will be prepared with antihistamines and possibly steroids as backup if your cat has a reaction. Cats with multiple or plaquelike tumors may have systemic (whole body) involvement (3).

Solitary mast cell tumors can be cured with surgery, but you must watch your cat carefully for any recurrence. Many cats will need follow-up radiation therapy.

Siamese cats—including cats that are only part Siamese, in our experience—have a predisposition to mast cell tumors.

Squamous Cell Cancers[1]

Squamous cell cancers make up 9 to 25 percent of all feline skin cancers (2). They are most commonly noted in cats nine to twelve years old. FIV-positive cats seem to have a higher risk, though this may be associated with the typical outdoor lifestyle of many FIV-positive cats (3).

Due to the solar influence (ultraviolet rays from the sun can be a factor just as in human skin cancers), white cats have a five to thirteen times greater risk than the average dark-colored cat (2, 3). Ears and noses are frequent sites for this cancer, so even dark-colored cats with white ears (especially tips) and noses are at some risk. Siamese and black cats do have a decreased risk of this one—in the Siamese, thanks to the dark points.

Owners may first notice this cancer as a "non-healing scratch." Be aware that such a sore on a light-colored area could be cancer.

Treatment for squamous cell cancers can vary. Surgery works well on ear tips but nasal tumors may need radiation therapy. In fact, 83 percent of the nasal squamous cell cancers respond to radiation treatments (2). Sadly, if your cat is FIV positive, she is more likely to suffer from the after-effects of radiation treatments, including the development of other skin cancers (3). **Cryotherapy** may or may not be effective.

Some cats have cancers that will respond to **intralesional** chemotherapy that involves injecting the medications directly into the cancer. One interesting area of treatment involves using photodynamic drugs (drugs activated by special lightwaves) injected into the tumor. These are primarily porphyrin derivatives (3).

---

1. See also chapter 4 for oral feline squamous cell cancer.

FELINE MAMMARY CANCER

Mammary, or breast, cancer is the third most common tumor in cats—accounting for 17 percent of all feline tumors (1). That translates into 25.5 cats with breast cancer per 100,000 female cats. (It is much rarer in male cats, as with humans. Statistics always make me question the ".5" cat and similar results as well!). While that may seem like a high rate, it is actually much lower than the incidence in humans or dogs.

Most of the cats with mammary cancer are older—the mean age being ten to twelve. Usually these are intact (not spayed) females. Unfortunately, about 80 percent of these cancers are malignant.

Signs You Can See
What an observant owner will notice first is a small lump along the **mammary chain** (this could be pea-sized). Right and left sides are equally at risk. Most cats quickly get multiple lumps, though solitary tumors are possible. The third and fourth glands in the line seem to be at higher risk (3).

Mammary tumors tend to adhere to the skin and eventually ulcerate. Sadly, there is an average of five months between the owner first noticing a lump and the cat having a veterinary exam (1). Remember, your home exam is your cat's first and best defense against serious cancers! Caught early, treatment is much more likely to be successful.

Diagnosis
Diagnosing breast cancer in your cat can be as simple as palpating a mass in the right area. Your veterinarian will need to differentiate cancer from benign **hyperplasia (**overgrowth, not related to cancer). Sometimes a needle aspirate will do the job. Your veterinarian will also carefully feel for an increase in size in any of the lymph nodes that drain the mammary glands.

It is important to take radiographs (x-rays) of your cat's chest at this time as well. Breast cancer in cats tends to spread to the local lymph nodes and lungs. It is estimated that over a quarter of the cats with breast cancer already have metastases to the lymph nodes at the time they are diagnosed (3).

Treatment

Surgery is the first line of treatment for mammary cancer in cats. Your veterinarian will take a wide area of normal tissue from around the affected glands and any suspect lymph nodes as well.

Many cats look like Frankenstein creations right after surgery, with incisions that go from their armpits all the way down to their groins! Do *not* be upset. As mentioned elsewhere, incisions heal side to side, not end to end. Also, it is much better to have a complete excision of the cancer than to leave some bad cells behind.

Questions remain over whether to spay an intact cat at the time of the cancer surgery. About 10 percent of feline mammary tumors are estrogen responsive, so for those tumors it certainly is important. While the association between spaying and breast cancer isn't quite as clear in cats as it is in dogs, unspayed cats have a seven times greater risk of developing this cancer to begin with (2). That plus the fact that older intact cats may develop life-threatening infections of the uterus called **pyometras** is enough to convince us that spaying is the way to go. Still, if your cat already has metastases and the surgery is being done to remove ulcerated tissue and try to keep your cat comfortable, it might make sense to skip the spay.

Chemotherapy may be done as a follow-up to surgery, but there have not been extensive protocols established. Doxorubicin and cyclophospahmide have been used (1). With these drugs, you need to watch for **anorexia** (loss of appetite) and for **myelodepression** (changes in the bone marrow causing decreased production of blood cells and platelets).

Prognosis

This is definitely one of those cancers that it pays to catch early. Staging and prognosis vary with the size of the original tumor and whether or not metastases are found. Also important is how well differentiated the cancer is. By *well differentiated* we mean, do the cancer cells look like breast cells specifically, or do they look like generic cancer cells? The more specialized, or well differentiated, the cells are, usually the better the prognosis.

As we mentioned, size is extremely important. Cats with solitary tumors less than two centimeters have the best chance of a long cancer-free life post surgery. Even a growth measured at two to three centimeters has a two-year prognosis as long as there aren't already extensive metastases. By the time a growth is 3 cm or larger, the expected survival time goes down to four to six months (1).

Prevention and Care

We do not have the big statistical evidence for cats that we do for dogs, which clearly suggests that spaying before puberty almost eliminates any chance of breast cancer. However, cats are reputed to have a sevenfold increased chance of breast cancer if they are not spayed before puberty—about six months of age in most cats (2). So spaying any cats not destined for breeding is highly recommended.

Also implicated in risk factors for the development of breast cancer in cats is the use of progesteronelike compounds for behavior and skin problems. Megestrol acetate was once widely used in cats but has fallen out of favor.

Cats who have undergone surgery for mammary cancer may be quite sore due to the extensive incisions. They will need careful post-op nursing, including pain medications to keep them comfortable. Encouraging eating with appetite stimulants and special treats is also important to speed healing. If your cat loves salmon steaks, this is one of the times I would cook her one!

Breed Predisposition

Siamese cats seem to be at increased risk for mammary cancer (1)—possibly even twice the risk of other cats. Domestic shorthairs also make the risk list, though with better prognoses overall than Siamese (3). Calicos in particular may be at increased risk (3). Remember, this does *not* mean that all calicos will get breast cancer at some point in their lives. Deb's twenty-one-year-old tort-with-a-tuxedo (calico) cat, Sam, who is sitting on the top of the computer, asked us to emphasize that, as she has never been sick a day in her life.

FELINE LYMPHOMA

Feline lymphoma is an important cancer in cats. There is increased risk in cats in the Northeast and with male cats (though that could relate to their increased likelihood of being feline-leukemia-virus [FELV] positive). Cats who are FELV-positive have a sixty times greater than average risk of developing lymphoma; cats who are FIV-positive have a five times greater risk of lymphoma; and if an unfortunate cat has both, the risk is eighty times greater than average (3)!

A full one-third of all feline tumors may be forms of lymphoma (1). Generally, about 200 cats of every 100,000 are at risk. Depending on the exact type of lymphoma, older cats or younger cats, FELV positive or negative, may all be victims.

Signs You Can See

Lymphoma has many forms—gastrointestinal tract (**alimentary**), spinal, and **mediastinal** being the most common. Signs you see will vary with the form.

Gastrointestinal lymphoma may be heralded by vomiting and diarrhea, but often cats simply show decreased appetite and weight loss. An unusual mass may be felt in the abdomen. This form is currently the most common type of lymphoma in cats and is seen in older cats (ten to twelve years of age) and is not associated closely with FELV status. Domestic shorthairs and Siamese may be at increased risk (3).

The most common site for this type of cancer is the small intestine (50 percent of the time); the stomach is second with about 25 percent of the cancers (1). So expect to see vomiting if your cat develops lymphoma in the stomach, with diarrhea more common if it is in the intestines. Lymphomas here may be single cancers or spread diffusely throughout the tissues. The diffuse versions are difficult to differentiate from inflammatory bowel disease.

Mediastinal lymphoma occurs in the lymph nodes in the front part of the chest (inside the chest cavity). This version is associated with young cats (under five years of age) who are FELV positive. Siamese cats and Oriental breeds in general seem to have an increased incidence (3). Cats with mediastinal lymphoma may have difficulty breathing, may regurgitate food (due to pressure on the esophagus), and may lose their appetite and have weight loss. Fluid (called pleural effusion) will build up in the chest, making it even harder to breathe. Sometimes the enlarged lymph nodes will put pressure on nerves, causing "Horner's Syndrome." In those cases you would see the "third eyelid" (normally a small white area in the corner of your cat's eye) covering much of your cat's eye (1)

Spinal or central nervous system lymphoma tends to show up in young (three- to four-year-old) male cats who are FELV positive (1). This is the most common central nervous system tumor after meningiomas (1). These cats often have problems using their hind legs. This may come on slowly and progress or show up very suddenly depending on how the tumor pushes on the spinal cord.

Less common versions of lymphoma may affect kidneys (renal lymphoma) or skin, or they may be multicentric. Renal lymphoma is often bilateral, so it affects both kidneys. These cats have signs of kidney failure—either drinking a lot or very little, urinating a lot or very little, often losing weight and having very little appetite.

The skin form of lymphoma tends to show up in older cats (ten to twelve years of age) who are FELV negative. This form and the multicentric form that may show up with enlarged lymph nodes visible are fairly uncommon.

Diagnosis

To diagnose lymphoma your cat will need a full workup. That will include a CBC and blood panel, along with testing for both FELV and FIV. A chest x-ray is important for mediastinal lymphoma but also to look for metastases. An abdominal ultrasound and/or x-rays can look for gastrointestinal lymphoma. Your cat may need a biopsy of intestinal tissues or a lymph node to diagnose lymphoma accurately. Inflammatory bowel disease can mimic intestinal lymphoma.

Your veterinarian may want to do a bone-marrow aspirate to check for cancer there as well and possibly even a spinal tap if your cat is showing weakness in the rear legs. Aspirating some fluid from the chest could tell if your cat has mediastinal lymphoma. Cats with lymphoma rarely have increased calcium levels.

Treatment

The exact treatment that your cat needs varies with the exact type of lymphoma she has. A cat with a solitary intestinal mass may just need surgery. Most forms are treated with a multiagent chemotherapy protocol.

Mediastinal lymphoma generally has a good response to chemotherapy (3), especially if your cat is FELV negative and doxorubicin is used. Doxorubicin can be quite toxic, but it is very effective in many cases.

In the rare cases of a localized lymphoma, radiation may be useful. Cats with spinal lymphoma tend to have a poor prognosis no matter what treatment is tried.

Cats with surgery or intense chemotherapy may not be able to eat on their own and may need to have feeding tubes placed. Diazepam (Valium®) can be used as an appetite stimulant.

Cats on chemotherapy may have some hair loss and you might notice the loss of whiskers. This hair usually all grows back, though the hair might be a different color or texture.

Prognosis

The prognosis for your cat can vary with the exact type of lymphocyte involved in the cancer. The location and whether or not your cat is FELV-positive are also factors. Cats with intestinal lymphoma that is one solitary mass may be cured with surgery. Even if the cancer is diffuse in the intestinal tract, if your cat responds well to initial treatment and gets a good first remission, the odds are better for a second remission (3).

Spinal lymphoma cases have a poor prognosis no matter what treatment is used. Mediastinal lymphoma is tough to treat, but even so, many cats respond fairly well and gain eight to ten weeks of quality life (1). (Remember, eight to ten weeks is relatively longer in a cat than a person.)

Prevention and Care

Keeping your cat indoors to prevent FELV and FIV infection is very important. Most lymphomas are influenced by the presence of those viruses.

Cats undergoing treatment, especially chemotherapy, may need nursing care or even a feeding tube to encourage them to eat.

Breed Predisposition

Siamese and domestic shorthairs have an increased risk of gastrointestinal lymphoma while Siamese and Oriental breeds also show an increased predisposition for mediastinal lymphoma. These risks may be associated with higher risk for FELV and FIV viruses in catteries (3).

FELINE LEUKEMIA

When we think of cancers and their causes, feline leukemia virus immediately comes to mind. This is a virus of the retrovirus family and is associated with a number of feline cancers. (Seventy percent of all cats with feline lymphoma are FELV positive [1]). Feline leukemia is considered to be the most common infectious disease of cats, with 3 percent of U.S. cats having this virus (22).

Just being exposed to this virus is not a guarantee of serious health problems, though. About 40 percent of all cats fight off this virus on their own. Some 30 percent die quickly from serious health problems associated with the virus (possibly acute nonlymphoid leukemia) (22). Of the other cats, some will eventually develop acute lymphoid leukemia and others will continue to keep the virus in their bodies—either as carriers or with the virus in a latent state—tucked away in tissues and not detectable by standard tests (1).

Signs You Can See

Cats with FELV disease often have nonspecific signs. They may not eat well, may lose weight, and may act lethargic and have fevers. Because the feline leukemia virus may suppress normal immunity, cats may show signs of other illnesses (1). Cats with acute lymphoid leukemia will have swollen lymph nodes (like dogs with lymphoma), but cats with "pure" leukemia will not.

Diagnosis

Diagnosis of feline leukemia often starts with two tests your veterinarian can run to look for the virus. One is the ELISA (enzyme linked immunosorbent assay) test and the other is the IFA (immunofluorescent assay), both of which look for the feline leukemia antigens. Remember that some cats fight off this virus on their own—so if you are using these tests as a screening (say for cats in a shelter), it makes sense to isolate positive but healthy cats and retest them in three months if possible. The ELISA test can be done on blood, saliva, or tears. If an ELISA test comes up positive, many veterinarians will recommend following up with an IFA test, using blood which is sent out to a laboratory.

The ELISA test can pick up feline leukemia exposure very early, but some cats will fight off this virus. The IFA test is more indicative of the virus remaining in the cat's body—either actively or sequestered (26).

Other diagnostic tests might include a general blood panel and a complete blood count, looking for any signs of abnormal cells and/or anemia. A bone marrow aspirate can be important for staging this disease (3). A PCR (polymerase chain reaction test) to specifically search for the virus is another definitive test, but not commonly done (1).

Treatment

Treatment for feline leukemia can be frustrating. Cats with the acute nonlymphoid leukemia often die within fourteen days of diagnosis (3). For these cats, blood transfusions and supportive care are important.

Cats with acute lymphoid leukemia (often with enlarged lymph nodes) do a bit better. Prednisone may help, though it can add to the immunosuppressive effect of the virus. Antibiotics may be important to fight off opportunistic infections. Other treatments aim at building up your cat's own immune system. Interferon, acemannan, and orthomolecular supplements (large doses of vitamins, especially vitamins A, C, and E) may all help keep your cat in good health even though they won't eliminate the virus (21).

Prognosis

As you may have realized, the prognosis of cats with feline leukemia virus varies greatly. Cats with the severe acute nonlymphoid type do very poorly. Cats with acute lymphoid leukemia may have seven to twenty-four months of good quality life (3). And of course, some cats will remain leukemia–virus positive but show no signs for many years, if ever.

Prevention and Care

Some studies have shown an association between young male cats and the feline leukemia virus. Because the virus is spread via saliva and blood, it is thought that young male cats who are out and about, getting into fights, are at greater risk. Certainly, keeping your cats indoors at all times and reducing their exposure to strange cats is a good idea.

If you plan to add a new cat to your family, consider doing feline leukemia testing *before* you bring her home. Screening cats ahead of time reduces the chances of spreading the virus.

Some studies show an association between pesticides and feline leukemia as well as many other cancers (22). Certainly, living with dandelions is preferable to dealing with cancers.

Because feline leukemia is a virus that some cats can fight off on their own, it makes sense to keep your cat in the best possible health. A good diet with a parasite-free, low-stress existence may help your cat to eliminate this virus if she gets exposed. A healthy immune system is a great defense!

There is a vaccination for feline leukemia virus. There are some controversies surrounding this vaccine—see the section on vaccine-associated sarcomas that follows. As with any vaccine, it is important to discuss with your veterinarian the potential risks of a disease and to customize the vaccination schedule. Cats who are totally indoors and not exposed to strange cats really don't need this vaccine. If your cat goes outside or you often foster cats, it might make sense to get it.

Breed Predisposition

There are no established breed predispositions.

VACCINE-ASSOCIATED SARCOMAS

Certainly, a scary prospect for many of us cat lovers is the fact that there has been some association between vaccinations and the development of cancers called sarcomas. This correlation came to light when veterinarians looked at the incidence of sarcomas in cats from 1988 to 1994. There was an eightfold increase in sarcomas and these seemed to be associated with vaccination sites (3). Estimates range from one in one thousand to one in ten thousand cats affected (22).

Looking closely at the studies, it became apparent that most of the sarcomas are associated with feline leukemia and rabies vaccines, especially the feline leukemia (22). At that time, more vaccines had been shifted from modified live to killed vaccines. In a killed vaccine, the virus is treated to make it nonvirulent. To stimulate enough immunity, compounds called *adjuvants* are added—aluminum being one of them (22). It was felt that the aluminum adjuvants were at least partially at fault and that the leukemia virus was a greater cause as that vaccine was given annually, while rabies is often given only every three years.

These sarcomas are very invasive cancers, eating into the tissues around them aggressively. They may occur after both intramuscular and subcutaneous vaccinations, though subcutaneous ones are more commonly associated with the problem (3). While we tend to think of these cancers as associated only with killed vaccinations, there have been cases of these sarcomas secondary to modified live vaccinations and to other injections—such as antibiotics (3).

Sadly, vaccination-associated sarcomas may show up months to even years later (3), leaving some families with long-term worries. There does seem to be a genetic predisposition for the development of these cancers and certainly any cat who has had one should not be vaccinated again (3). Clusters of this cancer can be seen in areas with many related susceptible cats.

Signs You Can See

This is a cancer that an astute family may pick up on early. Many cats will get a small reaction to the area where a vaccine is given. This small lump should not grow and should not persist for more than a month after vaccination (3). Any lumps present at vaccination sites after that time should be checked carefully.

Diagnosis

Diagnosing a vaccine-associated sarcoma starts with a good history—knowing that your cat received a vaccination in that location. Your veterinarian may choose to do a fine needle aspirate, taking some cells from the lump to look for abnormalities. She will also check for metastases, possibly doing blood work or at least taking chest x-rays.

Treatment

Many of these cancers are diagnosed and treated at the same time, with aggressive surgery. This is not the time to be squeamish about the size of the incision. While the cancer may appear to be a discrete lump, this type of cancer has long "fingers" that reach out into other tissues. Your veterinarian will be *incising* very widely around the mass. Remember, incisions heal side to side, not end to end.

The best results for treating vaccine-associated sarcomas seems to come from combining surgery with radiation—either pre- or post-surgery (27). The goal here is to combine surgery with removing the main mass and with radiation to catch any cells spreading through the other tissues. So far chemotherapy has not shown much success, either alone or in combination with other treatments.

Prognosis

Vaccine-associated sarcomas do not have a cure rate at this time. Most cats will have a recurrence, despite aggressive surgery and even radiation. Still, many cats gain a year or more of quality life with treatment.

Prevention and Care

The American Veterinary Medical Association, the American Animal Hospital Association, and the Association of Feline Practitioners formed a task force to deal with the problem of vaccine-associated sarcomas (28).

Their guidelines include trying to reduce the number of vaccinations your cat may need—for example, if she is an indoor-only cat, she may not need a vaccine for feline leukemia. Do not give any of the optional vaccines such as for Giardia or ringworm unless absolutely necessary. Reduce the frequency of vaccines—while many vaccines used to be given yearly, now most are given every three years or even less frequently.

Try not to give multiple vaccines at the same site (27). It is suggested that feline leukemia vaccines be given in the left rear leg while rabies be given in the right rear leg. Those are the vaccines most commonly associated with the sarcomas, and with those sites, amputation is a possibility for treatment.

Totally avoiding vaccines may not be a safe move; panleukopenia (feline distemper) and rabies are often fatal diseases. And remember, fortunately many cats never have any problem. Deb's cat Samantha is at least twenty-one years old and despite having had many vaccines over the years has remained sarcoma free.

Breed Predisposition

While no breed predisposition has become apparent for these sarcomas, some cats do seem to have a genetic predisposition and certain lines of cats may have a greater risk (3).

FELINE HYPERTHYROIDISM/THYROID CANCER

There will be those who argue that hyperthyroidism doesn't really belong in a book about cancer, but most cases of hyperthyroidism (increased thyroid hormones) in cats are caused by tumors—usually benign adenomas, but occasionally carcinomas.

Apparently, around the 1970s there was suddenly an increase in feline thyroid tumors that produced hormones (3). These cancers tend to appear in older cats and may produce extra T3 and T4 thyroid hormones.

Signs You Can See

When you notice that your older cat has switched from sedate seniorhood to wild kittenhood, suspect a thyroid problem. Families frequently notice weight loss despite a *big* appetite (even opening cupboards and tearing open food packages!) Your cat who used to spend her days soaking up the sun on a windowsill is now tearing around the house, playing, running up and down stairs, and so on.

Other cats don't show these dramatic changes but are more active. Some families notice an increase in vomiting, some panting even when it is cool, and hair loss.

Very carefully palpating the neck area may reveal a lump or nodule where the thyroid is located—lift up the cat's chin and carefully feel underneath. Thyroid tumors may occur on just one side or on both.

Diagnosis

Diagnosing a thyroid cancer involves doing some bloodwork. Your veterinarian will do a full blood panel to verify that kidneys and liver are okay, but will also add a test for thyroid hormone levels, primarily T4. If all the signs point to a thyroid cancer but the T4 level is normal, your veterinarian may do some extra tests to verify thyroid responses. Almost all cats show an increased T4 level, however.

Many veterinarians now also check blood pressure (high in hyperthyroid cats) and possibly check an echocardiogram and EKG to make sure the heart is not enlarged and is beating normally (35).

Treatment

There is a smorgasbord of treatments for thyroid cancers in cats, but also some definite cautions. The increased blood flow from the T4 cells and high blood pressure may cover up renal (kidney) failure. Completely treating the thyroid problem may shift your cat over into life-threatening kidney failure. For this reason, many veterinarians now start off with a "test" treatment of a medication called *methimazole* before any other more definitive care (3).

Methimazole is a medication that reduces thyroid hormone output. It must be given daily and for the rest of your cat's life unless you go on to surgery or radiation treatment. For cats with underlying kidney disease, this may be the treatment of choice. Luckily, newer versions of this drug are being produced by compounding pharmacies that allow you to put a gel in your cat's ear as opposed to giving her a pill daily. A cat on long-term methimazole will need periodic blood tests to check her blood counts and her thyroid hormone levels.

Another option is surgery to remove the cancerous gland. Your veterinary surgeon will be extra careful to avoid damaging the parathyroid gland (very small gland next to the thyroid) that regulates calcium metabolism. If the parathyroid is damaged your cat will need supplements to help with calcium control. Calcium regulation problems can be life threatening, so many veterinarians hospitalize a cat for a few days after surgery just to verify that the parathyroids are fine. Even if your cat develops a parathyroid problem, many cats heal the damage in a month or so (3). Still, surgery can be a quick and definitive treatment. Deb's parents had a fourteen-year-old cat with a thyroid tumor who lived for three years after surgery.

The third option is to use radioactive iodine to wipe out the thyroid cancer. The thyroid gland tends to concentrate iodine, so giving 131-I (a radioactive iodine compound) sends the iodine directly to the thyroid and destroys the cells there. A few cats may end up hypothyroid (low thyroid hormone levels) after treatment and need supplementation, but most cats do fine.

A drawback to this treatment is that only certain facilities offer it, because strict guidelines covering radioactive material must be followed. That includes boarding your cat at the facility for seven to twenty-five days. Your cat's urine and feces may shed radioactive material so for *your* safety she has to stay at the facility until the level of radiation goes below safety requirements.

Keep in mind that most of these cats are older and may have underlying disease that will influence what treatment can be used and how successful treatment will be. Heart and kidney damage are the most serious related problems that can be life threatening.

Prognosis

For the benign thyroid adenomas, the prognosis for cats caught early, before underlying damage to heart or kidneys, is excellent. In one study, 34 percent of the cats treated were still alive and doing well four years after radioactive iodine therapy (3). Once the heart or kidneys have been damaged, this damage tends to be the cause of death, rather than the thyroid tumor itself.

If your cat is one of the unlucky ones who gets a carcinoma (about 2 percent of all cats with thyroid problems), the prognosis is much graver. Metastasis to the lungs or lymph nodes is common (3). Surgery may not be successful because of invasiveness. Still, even for these cats, use of radiation or chemotherapy may help, at least short term.

Prevention and Care

Living in an environment with smokers increases risk, so we have yet another reason to quit smoking (3). Use of flea products may or may not be a factor (3). Some studies have shown that cats eating mostly canned food, using litter, or being indoor cats may have an increased risk (3). Those statistics need to be evaluated carefully though, as indoor cats are more likely to live longer (so live long enough to develop a thyroid problem) and may also be more likely to be diagnosed as their owners can more easily note any changes.

Once your cat is diagnosed, you need to follow any medication schedules carefully (methimazole MUST be given daily if you are using that), encourage eating to keep up your cat's weight and strength, and stay on top of rechecks for blood tests, and heart and kidney function evaluations.

Breed Predispositions

Himalayans and Siamese have a lower risk of developing thyroid cancers. Relatives of cats who do get thyroid cancer (mostly domestic shorthairs and longhairs) are at increased risk, so there may be a genetic predisposition among certain cat families.

SUMMARY

- Skin cancers make up a large percentage of cancers cats can get: 50-65% are malignant.
- You can possibly reduce mammary tumors by spaying your cat before she is six months old.
- You can greatly reduce the risk of feline lymphoma by limiting your cat's exposure to outdoor cats.
- You can reduce the potential of vaccine related sarcomas by following the vaccination protocols as put forth by the American Association of Feline Practitioners.

CHAPTER
4

Less Common Cancers

IN THIS CHAPTER
- Learn about some of the more uncommon cancers that affect dogs and cats.
- Learn how skin cancers (melanomas) affect both dogs and cats.
- Learn how to help prevent certain cancers from occurring.

This chapter deals with some of the less common cancers. The fact that they are not seen frequently means very little when *your* pet has one of these. Some of these are benign cancers, others are quite malignant. Ideally, you will find information to guide your decision making.

Case Study

Riser was a happy go lucky four-year-old yellow Labrador Retriever when Linda W. found an egg-sized lump on his shoulder. He suffered from epilepsy and was on medications for that, but was otherwise fine.

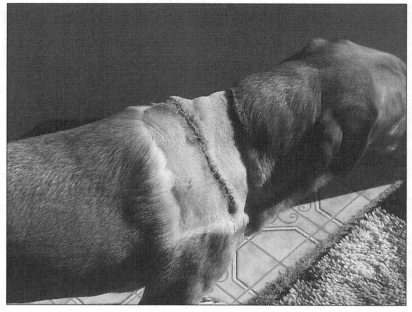

Riser's scar is not as bad as it looks.
Wounds heal side-to-side, not end-to-end.

Surprisingly, the lump would wax and wane, shrinking down to al-
most nothing, and then blowing up into a large mass. It was not painful
to touch or ulcerated. Linda would schedule a vet appointment, and then it
would almost disappear. Finally, after a couple of weeks, Linda managed
to get Riser in when his growth was large.

Riser's veterinarian did surgery and sent off a biopsy even though the
lump was down to pea size by the time of surgery. The biopsy came back as
a Grade II mast cell tumor, but with clean margins. The fact that it was a
mast cell tumor explains the changes in size. When mast cells are irritated
(by being touched or from Riser scratching at it), they release histamine
and cause local swelling. When the histamine wears off, the swelling goes
down. Other owners whose pets have had mast cell tumors report that they
rub a tiny lump, and almost immediately it gets larger and red in color.

Since the margins (edges of the surgery area) were clean, with no sign of cancer cells, no further treatment was done. Unfortunately, six months later another lump appeared at the same site. Riser went back in for surgery—a bit more dramatic this time. Riser's report came back as a Grade II mast cell tumor again, but this time, despite the even larger surgery site, there were cancer cells right out to the margins. There was concern that he might have metastases too.

At this point, Riser went on to see a veterinary oncologist. For a complete staging to plan his further treatment carefully, Riser also had a bone marrow evaluation. That test left him a bit sore, but he was able to compete in obedience in the utility class the following weekend.

When all Riser's preliminary testing was done, it was decided that follow-up radiation made the most sense. Riser flew through his radiation therapy—it pays to be a young Lab. His only side effect was hair loss at the

Cancer didn't slow Riser down.

treatment sites that took about four months to regrow and came in a bit darker.

Riser went almost four years before his cancer returned. This time, Linda found a growth at his shoulder and another on his hip. It was decided to go with radiation again, though this would be Riser's last round of radiation therapy, as he was nearing his lifetime safe exposure limit. Additional radiation treatments might actually increase the chances of cancer or do too much damage to normal tissues.

A few months later, Riser had an enlarged lymph node that had an inconclusive biopsy report. In the summer of 2003, seven years after his initial bout with cancer, Riser had another small Grade II mast cell tumor removed from his belly. As of this writing (June 2004), Riser is twelve years old and just retired from competing in American Kennel Club (AKC) agility trials.

Riser's hair grew back and it's hard to tell he's a cancer survivor.

Despite his cancer, Riser competed in obedience, achieving national ranking; earned a hunting title; and participated in agility. At the Labrador Retriever Club national competition in 2003, Riser received recognition as the "Dog for All Reasons." Though technically retired, Riser still does some fieldwork and stays in shape doing agility at home.

As Linda says, "Riser has truly been a miracle dog, the name coined by his doctors. Bad things happen to good dogs. Riser is the sweetest dog I have ever owned and never deserved all this."

Riser's case gives us an example of a dog who has handled cancer treatment with aplomb, continuing with most of his activities and leading a long, active life. His excellent care and the thorough home exams by Linda to detect problems early have contributed to his success.

FELINE MENINGIOMA

Of all cancers, the ones that scare us the most are brain tumors. Fortunately, some brain tumors aren't an automatic death sentence. Meningiomas in cats can be a treatable disease. These tumors arise from the covering over the brain (called **meninges**). While they can grow into the brain tissue, normally they cause signs by simply putting pressure on brain cells. This is the most common type of brain tumor in cats.

Meningiomas are almost always cancers of older cats, and males in particular are predisposed (3). These tend to be slow-growing tumors, but the clinical signs may show up acutely and without much warning.

Signs You Can See

Since meningiomas are slow-growing tumors you may see some gradual changes in your cat. Behavior may change, with your cat becoming aggressive or lethargic (depending on which area of the brain is feeling the pressure). Signs may be a subtle as a decrease in purring (1).

Some cats show an increase in vocalizations, may hide more, or may sit staring off into space. Vision problems may become apparent, and about 50 percent of the cats show circling behaviors (tending to walk in a circle). Sixty to 80 percent of the cats with meningioma eventually show **paresis** (weakness) of one or more limbs. Rarely, a cat may have seizures. Many of these signs can appear as the result of age changes as well, so diagnosis can be tricky. Metastases are rare, so normally there are no changes resulting from spread to the liver, lungs, or other tissues.

Diagnosis

Diagnosing a meningioma can be complicated. Your veterinarian will need a careful history from you—detailing what changes you noticed, when, and so on. Then your vet needs to do a complete physical exam including a **neurologic** exam. Ideally, your cat will have special imaging to her head, such as an **MRI (magnetic resonance imaging)** or a **CT (computerized tomography) scan**. Plain x-rays are not usually helpful. An accurate diagnosis may require referral to a specialist.

Treatment

Treating a meningioma almost always requires surgery. Radiation may help, but the best course of action is surgery to remove the mass and relieve pressure on the brain. A successful surgery can lead to rapid improvement of clinical signs and may even restore vision that was lost from tumor effects.

Before surgery is done, it is important to know the extent of the mass. This is where the specialized imaging becomes important. Your cat's surgeon needs to know as accurately as possible just where the tumor is, if it is single or has invaded brain tissue (not a good sign), and if the tumor is close to the surface so it can be more easily removed without disrupting healthy tissues. If your cat is already showing severe neurologic signs or has other serious health problems, surgery may not be a reasonable alternative.

It is important to realize that this is very delicate, complicated surgery. You need an experienced surgeon with a well-trained team to assist and the necessary technological backup. Postoperative care is intensive. The risk of **hemorrhage** during the postoperative period is great. In one study, eight of forty-two cats died in the postoperative period, mostly from hemorrhage (2). Even with a successful surgery, your cat may not recover fully.

Prognosis

With a successful surgery, many cats have a good long-term survival prognosis. For pets with cancer, that translates into a year or more of good quality life. I realize a year doesn't sound like much at first, but remember that cats are not humans with long lifespans, and most of these are older cats to begin with. If the cancer does recur, radiation may help gain some more quality time.

Prevention and Care

There are no known related causes of meningiomas. Your best bet for these tumors is early detection, so that surgery can be done early and be less traumatic because of a smaller mass and less residual damage to the brain. Any changes in your cat's behavior should send off warning signals. Even if it isn't brain cancer, it might be another health problem that early treatment could help.

Breed Predispositions

Domestic shorthairs are the main category of cats with meningiomas. Among the purebreds, Persians seem to be the most common (3).

UVEAL MELANOMA—CANINE

The **uvea** is the vascular layer of the eye—the iris, choroids, and ciliary body. This layer is right under the sclera or tough outer coating and is usually pigmented.

The most common primary cancer appearing here is the melanoma, a cancer growing from the pigment cells. As might be expected, these tumors are often pigmented, but not always. Since this is a heavily vascular area, there may be secondary tumors that have spread via the blood system.

Uveal melanomas are more common in older dogs, especially those over seven years of age.

Signs You Can See

Dogs with uveal melanoma may have inflammation of the eye, **hyphema** or blood visible in the eye, or a secondary glaucoma with increased pressure, loss of vision, and possibly permanent damage to the eye. So your dog may have trouble seeing; have a very red, sore eye; and seem to be in pain or depressed. In my opinion, *any* change in an eye—squinting, sudden tearing, or other symptoms—is an emergency!

Diagnosis

Diagnosing a uveal melanoma (or any **ocular** tumor) is dependent on a very careful ophthalmologic examination. Your own veterinarian may diagnose this or refer you to a veterinary ophthalmologist for confirmation of the diagnosis. Transillumination, using lights to look across the eye, may highlight a problem. Ultrasound of the eye is becoming more common and should help in diagnosis.

Treatment

If treatment is needed, **enucleation,** or removal of the eye, is recommended. Removing the eye prevents local invasion of the tumor into other tissues, prevents metastases, and may help to relieve pain (2). Laser therapy has been tried but with variable success (1). You still need to have your dog checked periodically for any signs of metastases.

Prognosis

Most uveal melanomas in dogs are classifed as benign on the basis of their **mitotic index.** This is determined by looking at sections of removed tissue under a microscope to see how fast the cells are replicating (1). In general, the darker growths are more likely to be benign. Overall, about 4 percent of uveal melanomas have metastases, but of the growths classified as malignant, about 25 percent will have spread at the time of diagnosis and treatment (1).

These tumors are evaluated by their speed of growth and aggressiveness in invading local tissues as well.

Prevention And Care

Exposure to radium may lead to an increase in uveal melanomas, but that is fairly unusual in dogs.

Breed Predisposition

No breed predispositions were found, though some veterinarians feel Labrador Retrievers and Golden Retrievers are over-represented.

UVEAL MELANOMAS—FELINE

Uveal melanomas in cats are almost always considered to be malignant tumors, though many are slow growing. These are cancers of the **vascular** portion of the eye—the iris, ciliary body, and choroids. Since these are very vascular tumors, it is easy for them to metastasize via blood vessels.

This is the primary **ocular** tumor in cats (2). Uveal melanomas tend to occur mostly in cats who are ten years of age or older.

Signs You Can See

Cats with iris or uveal melanomas will have pigment changes in their eyes. (Benign pigment changes can occur, as well, especially in older orange cats, so don't panic right away [1].) Sometimes pigment changes are very mild.

You might notice that your cat's eye is red or inflamed; also, glaucoma is often seen as a secondary problem. Most commonly, these melanomas only show up in one eye. Consider any change in your cat's eye such as squinting, tearing, and so on, an emergency.

Diagnosis

Your own veterinarian may diagnose this cancer by a careful eye exam or may refer you to a veterinary ophthalmologist for confirmation. An ultrasound, **MRI**, or **CT scan** can be very helpful in determining if the cancer has been aggressively invading local tissues (3). Careful **thoracic** (chest) **radiographs** (x-rays) should be taken to look for spread of the cancer.

Your veterinarian will be trying to distinguish between this cancer and benign pigment and cysts.

Treatment

Enucleation (removal of the eye by surgery) is the most common treatment for uveal melanomas in cats. If caught very early, this might prevent spread and will certainly relieve pain. Fifty-five to 66 percent of the cats will already have metastases at the time of surgery (1). Radiation can be palliative and help reduce pain for cats with locally invasive cancer.

Newer laser techniques may be suitable for removing some of these tumors in cats.

If your cat is found to have metastases, chemotherapy may help. Carboplatin and doxorubicin are the drugs most frequently mentioned for treating the metastases. Signs of metastases can include weight loss, lethargy, breathing problems, and abdominal distension. If your cat has many of these signs, it may be reasonable to simply try to control pain and give her a good quality of life for her time remaining.

Prognosis

The prognosis for cats with uveal melanomas is not good. This is an aggressive cancer, and if there are already signs of invasiveness or metastases when your cat is diagnosed, the condition is grave. Even if only the iris and ciliary body appear to be infected, survival is about one year (3).

Prevention and Care

There have been some cases of uveal melanomas in cats with experimental cases of feline sarcoma virus. In these cases, enucleation led to an increase in metastases (1). There has not been an association shown between this virus and spontaneous cancer, however.

The most important thing to remember if your cat has an ocular tumor is that it can be very painful. Radiation and/or pain medications may be necessary to keep your cat comfortable.

Breed Predispositions

Persian cats seem to have an increased susceptibility to uveal melanomas. This only applies to the ocular melanomas, not the skin versions.

CANINE MELANOMAS IN THE MOUTH AND TOES

Besides the eyes, melanomas are tumors that are found in the mouths of dogs and sometimes on the feet, especially the toes. While melanomas in or on the skin of dogs are often benign, in the mouth these cancers are generally malignant. There are some interesting breed differences. In Doberman Pinschers and Miniature Schnauzers

75 percent of melanomas are benign. Miniature Poodles, on the other hand, have 85 percent malignant melanomas (1). About 30 percent of the toe and nailbed melanomas are also malignant.

Signs You Can See

Dogs with any type of cancer in their mouths will often drool quite a bit. Your dog may act as if his mouth is painful—either to touch or when trying to eat or drink. Many dogs are in pain and will resist it if you try to open their mouths (remember that some dogs don't like having their mouths opened to begin with).

If you can look inside the mouth, you may see a dark or black growth. Melanomas will sometimes be unpigmented as well, and these growths can appear whitish in color. Sometimes masses will have ulcerated, leaving a reddish, raw area.

Melanomas on toes are usually pigmented and initially appear as swollen areas. If untreated, these growths also ulcerate, leaving non-healing sore areas.

Diagnosis

Melanomas may be diagnosed by needle biopsies, or, in the case of toes, removal of the whole toe. With the toes, it makes more sense to remove the whole toe than to take a biopsy and possibly stir up the cancer cells.

Treatment

Treatment for these cancers almost always involves surgery. With the toe cancers, removal of the toe may even be curative if surgery is done before any metastases have spread. Follow-up radiation can also be done.

While it sounds very drastic, removing part of the jaw works quite well for many dogs. (See the section on oral cancers later in this chapter.) Again, follow-up radiation and/or chemotherapy may be recommended if any metastases are suspected.

Gene therapy is currently being suggested for oral melanomas (1).

Prognosis

Sadly, even with drastic surgery, the prognosis is not spectacular. Survival times post surgery range from nine months (2) to one year (1). Still, a year of quality life is certainly an achievement.

Prevention and Care

With a major oral surgery, your dog will need nursing care and possibly diet changes. For a toe removal, some of her activities may need to be changed or dropped. However, many dogs can still run with agility with toes removed. Pain medications can be important for both oral and toe cancer patients.

Breed Predisposition

Dogs with lots of black pigment do seem to be at an increased risk for melanomas. Breeds often mentioned are Cocker Spaniels, Boston Terriers, and Scottish Terriers (22).

CANINE SQUAMOUS CELL CARCINOMAS OF THE TOES

Along with the melanomas already discussed, dogs are susceptible to squamous cell carcinomas of their toes. This cancer is generally seen in medium to large breed dogs, especially if they are basically black in color (1). This is a cancer of older dogs, with most being nine years or older when the cancer is diagnosed.

While considered somewhat aggressive, the rate of metastasis is not high. Still, based on cell criteria, these should be considered at least potentially malignant cancers and must be distinguished from toe melanomas.

Signs You Can See

You may notice a swollen toe, which may be red and inflamed. Most are quite sore, and many dogs will limp or be lame. Sometimes people notice the growth because their dog is suddenly licking at her foot or toe more than usual. Normally just one toe will be involved, but some dogs have multiple toe involvement. If your dog has had a toe removed due to a squamous cell carcinoma, it is important to continue to check her feet. The cancer may show up in another toe at a later time. More than one dog has lost two or even three toes to this cancer eventually.

Diagnosis

Often the best way to diagnose these toe cancers is to remove the toe and then send the tissues to a pathologist. Some veterinarians may do a needle biopsy first.

Treatment

The ideal treatment is to amputate the toe. In the rare case of metastasis to the lungs, chemotherapy, such as the drug cisplatin, may be helpful (3).

Prognosis

At least 40 percent of dogs with squamous cell carcinomas of the toe survive for two years after diagnosis and treatment (3). That is a significant amount of time, considering that many of these dogs are older to begin with.

Prevention and Care

Following surgery such as toe amputation, you may need to adjust your dog's activities, though many dogs can run despite a missing toe.

It is very important to provide pain medication post surgery, as your dog's foot can be quite sore.

Breed Predisposition

Black Labrador Retrievers and black Standard Poodles (1) seem to have a predisposition to these cancers, which may be color related. Giant Schnauzers (most of whom are black in color) definitely have a predisposition to this cancer. Many of them will have multiple cancerous toes (1, 3).

TRANSITIONAL CELL CARCINOMA—CANINE

Transitional cell carcinoma is the most common **urinary tract** tumor in dogs. Older female dogs are at greatest risk, especially for growths in the bladder. Most victims of this cancer are ten or older. This can be quite an aggressive cancer—being locally invasive and spreading via metastases to the lymph nodes and the lungs.

Signs You Can See

Families often notice their dog straining to urinate, urinating more frequently than normal, or even having **hematuria** (blood in the urine). Rarely, a dog may become obstructed, so that the tumor blocks the flow of urine, and nothing comes out while your dog tries to urinate. These signs could all indicate a bladder infection or bladder stones as well, so do *not* panic. If you note signs like these, you should at the very least try to collect a urine sample to take to your veterinarian. Ideally, take your dog along, too.

Pressure on the abdomen may be painful for some dogs, or they may walk with an uncomfortable gait.

As with virtually all cancers, the sooner a problem is noted and treated the better. It pays to walk your dog at least once a day even if you have a fenced yard, or at least go outside with your dog so you can observe whether she has any problems eliminating.

Diagnosis

Diagnosing transitional cell carcinomas relies on a good physical exam coupled with a full **urinalysis** and most likely some imaging and blood work. A physical exam may show pain in the abdomen and, though rare, a palpable mass.

Urine samples will often have blood cells (even if the urine doesn't look red, as the urine may dilute out the blood). Cells that fight inflammation and infection may also be present. Again, those findings could also occur with a bladder infection. About 30 percent of the time, cancer cells are found in the sample (2). Obviously, that could give you a diagnosis.

Blood work could show anemia and increased enzyme activity.

Even with a diagnosis of cancer, you will need imaging techniques to help decide if surgery is a possibility and exactly where the tumor(s) is located. Plain x-rays may not show very much, because this is a soft tissue (as opposed to bone) problem. Usually a contrast study is done with dye and/or air to try and outline any growth and see exactly where in the bladder or urinary tract it is located. About 90 percent of all bladder cancers can be and are diagnosed by contrast radiographs (2).

Ultrasound is helpful, and sometimes **cystoscopy** (putting a small viewing optic up into the bladder) can be useful, especially for getting a biopsy.

X-rays should be taken of the chest to look for lung metastases as well.

Treatment

Treatment depends greatly on exactly where the cancer is located. If it is where the **ureters** (tubes running from the kidney to the bladder funneling urine) enter the bladder or where urine leaves the bladder, surgery is more difficult. Surgery to reroute the path of urine, as can be done in people, is difficult for dogs, who don't handle collection bags well. Loss of the muscles or nerves that control urination could lead to a pet who leaks all the time, develops urine scald, and is very mentally stressed.

Still, surgery remains the first line of action, especially if the cancer is confined to a small area of the bladder. Up to 80 percent of the bladder can be removed successfully depending on the exact location of the growth (1).

Surgery may be combined with radiation. This could be done intraoperatively or as follow-up.

Chemotherapy is also being studied. Cisplatin is the drug most commonly used, but it can cause renal (kidney) toxicity. Piroxicam (a nonsteroidal anti-inflammatory drug used for arthritis) shows some promise. This is an example of how veterinary **oncologists** are continually exploring new uses of current medications to try and treat pets with cancer as well as searching for new treatments.

Prognosis

This is a nasty and aggressive cancer. Most dogs have advanced disease by the time they are diagnosed. That could mean a large growth, a spread to lymph nodes and/or lungs, or all three. Despite surgery, many dogs have metastases or recurrence of their tumors in a year. Again, the key to long-term survival is early detection, diagnosis, and thorough treatment.

Prevention and Care

Much more work has been done on exposure risk in people than in dogs. People who smoke, those who work with pesticides, hairdressers (working around chemicals), and petroleum workers all have an increased risk for this type of cancer (2). With dogs, risk factors isolated include obesity (a problem in many older females) and the use of certain topical insecticides (such as **organophosphates**), which is dose-related (2). Try to avoid petroleum distillates (products derived from petroleum).

Cyclophospamide is a chemotherapy drug that can, as a side effect, increase the risk of transitional cell carcinoma. Tryptophan (an **amino acid**) and its metabolites are also considered risk factors (1).

Dogs with transitional cell carcinoma need to be encouraged to drink and must have good nutrition to help fight the cancer and keep their blood counts normal. They may need pain medications and help with their hygiene because of urine leaking and scald.

Breed Predisposition
No breed predispositions were noted.

LIVER TUMORS—CANINE AND FELINE

Tumors found in the livers of dogs and cats are most commonly metastatic—that is, they have spread there from a primary cancer located somewhere else. Dogs are 2.5 times more likely to have metastatic liver tumors than primary liver tumors. When pets do have primary liver cancers, dogs tend to get malignant cancers while cats most often have benign primary liver cancers (9)

There are many different types of liver cancers—they vary with the exact cell types that becomes cancerous and include not only liver cells but also **bile duct** cells. Of course, metastatic liver tumors will show the cell type of the primary cancer they came from. Hemangiosarcoma is a tumor that often metastasizes to the liver.

Signs You Can See
The liver is considered part of the digestive tract, and cancers in the liver tend to have signs related to that. The liver not only helps with di-

gestion, but it also filters out some toxins and produces some proteins and vitamins. It is an important source of the blood factors that help with clotting. Your pet might vomit, show weight loss, or drink and urinate more than normal.

Some pets will develop **ascites**, or fluid build-up in the abdomen. This can also occur with some heart problems. In these cases, your pet may appear to be gaining weight, but is actually a skinny animal with a large fluid-filled belly.

In some cases, you and your veterinarian may be able to feel a large mass in your pet's abdomen. This is easier in cats than dogs. Some pets will develop **icterus** or **jaundice,** and you will be able to see a yellow color when you carefully check their eyes, gums, or inner ears. Rarely, a pet will build up toxins and have seizures.

Diagnosis

Blood work is quite helpful in diagnosing liver tumors. The CBC (complete blood count) will often indicate anemia. It is also possible that the platelets and white blood cells will be increased. The blood panel will show an increase in liver enzymes, especially with primary liver cancers. A special bile-acids test may be done to confirm the liver involvement. Cats tend to show **azotemia**—an increase in **BUN** or **blood urea nitrogen**. New on the horizon is a blood test for alpha feto protein, which might be a marker for liver cancers (9)

Your veterinarian may want to do a **coagulation** profile. This series of blood tests checks to be sure that your pet has normal clotting ability. While this information isn't diagnostic for liver cancer, it is important to know before any carrying out any treatment such as surgery.

An ultrasound may be able to identify a liver tumor and can be used to carefully guide a needle biopsy for exact diagnosis.

Treatment

The ideal treatment for liver cancer is surgery. This can be curative if only one lobe of the liver is cancerous and if that lobe is on the left side (it is easier to do surgery that way). If multiple lobes of the liver are involved or the cancer is spread throughout the liver, surgery may not be feasible. The same guidelines hold true if the liver cancer is metastatic and not primary.

Veterinarians are looking at cryotherapy, laser surgery, radiation, and various chemotherapy protocols to find better ways to treat liver cancers.

Prognosis

Prognosis varies greatly with the extent of the cancer and whether it is primary or metastatic. To truly treat a metastatic cancer, you must take care of the primary mass as well as the metastatic ones. Bile duct carcinoma is the number one liver cancer in cats, and it is very aggressive, with a grave prognosis. Over 80 percent of cancers of this type have spread by the time they are diagnosed.

Prevention and Care

Pets who have suffered from liver cancer may need special dietary care for the rest of their lives. **Trematode** infections (trematodes are parasites that tend to live in wet or marshy areas) may be associated with liver cancers (9). Routine fecal testing and watching for any signs of parasite infections are good ideas, especially if you live in a wet or marshy area.

Breed Predispositions

Male Schnauzers and male dogs in particular may be predisposed to liver cancers. Female cats and Labrador Retrievers are more likely to have bile duct carcinomas than other pets (9).

FELINE ORAL SQUAMOUS CELL CARCINOMA

About 10 percent of all feline cancers occur in the mouth. Of those **oral** cancers, 60 to 70 percent are squamous cell carcinomas (34). This is the same type of cancer seen on the ears of white cats (see feline skin cancers in chapter 3), but it acts differently in the mouth.

Oral squamous cell carcinomas tend to be cancers of older cats— ten years and up. A common location in the mouth is at the base of the tongue. Researchers have suspected this might be due to the dedicated grooming habits of cats. Your cat might be licking and grooming carcinogens off her coat that then get trapped under the tongue (27). Squamous cell carcinomas can also invade the bones of the jaw or spread to the bones from the gum tissues.

Signs You Can See

Cats with cancers in their mouths tend to drool, have trouble eating, or not want to eat; they may have a bad odor from the mouth. If the growth is large and located toward the outside of the mouth, a swelling might be obvious. Some cats will be unable to shut their mouths completely due to the tumor size. You may notice your cat going to the food or water bowls, but simply sitting there, as it is too painful to try to eat or drink.

Since this type of cancer may cause ulcers to become necrotic (*necrosis* means death of tissues), you may notice a red tinge (from blood) to the drool. If you look into your cat's mouth, you can almost always clearly see a growth.

Some cats first show irritation of the gums and even loose teeth (3). Squamous cell carcinomas may be detected early during dental work—another good reason for top preventive care!

Diagnosis

Diagnosing squamous cell carcinoma of the mouth usually involves doing a needle aspirate or taking a biopsy. Often this cancer is definitively diagnosed after a radical surgery has been done to remove the growth. X-rays may show damage to the bones of the jaw or skull. Ultrasound may also show changes in the skull and tissues of the mouth.

Treatment

Treatment for squamous cell carcinoma of the mouth almost always involves surgery. This could be as drastic as removing part of the jaw or tongue or could simply be to reduce the tumor mass so that radiation will be more successful. Antibiotics alone may gain your cat eight weeks by clearing up secondary infections and inflammation, but that is all. With surgery and follow-up radiation, some cats have done well for up to thirty-six months (27). One successful plan involves surgery of the growth and surrounding area, removal of local lymph nodes, and radiation. This plan may give your cat eleven or more months of comfort (3).

So far, chemotherapy has not been particularly helpful, but some work has been done with mitoxantrone (27).

Since surgery may be quite extensive, many cats will need a feeding tube placed for postoperative care. This requires a dedicated caretaker to keep the tubes clean and follow feeding instructions carefully. Most cats tolerate the tubes (which are placed into the stomach and then sutured outside to the skin for treatment access) extremely well.

Prognosis

Prognosis varies greatly with how large the growth is and whether it is in an area where it can be removed surgically. Sadly, many cats are only diagnosed after the cancer has infiltrated many tissues.

Prevention and Care

Interestingly, this cancer in cats has been associated with exposure to tobacco smoke (32). Another good reason to kick that habit.

If you choose to go with hospice care, your cat will need careful attention to her eating and drinking. Food and water may need to be room temperature and food may have to be slurried. Giving medications orally (such as antibiotics and pain medications) may be painful or very tricky. You may need training in giving injections.

Breed Predispositions

There are no known breed predispositions. Most cats with squamous cell carcinoma of the mouth are domestic shorthairs or domestic longhairs (3).

CANINE MAST CELL CANCER (MASTOCYTOMA)

Canine mast cell tumors are the most common skin tumor in dogs (1). You may also hear this cancer called "mastocytoma." This cancer is known as one of the great deceivers. It can show up with a wide range of appearances and clinical signs. Virtually any skin growth could be a mast cell tumor. These growths may show up at any age, but are more common in middle-aged to older dogs.

Mast cells are cells that are involved in immune response, especially allergic type reactions. One of the substances they release is histamine and many of the signs seen with this type of cancer are related to the histamine (think of the signs that drive you to take an "antihistamine").

Signs You Can See

The skin growths of mast cell tumors can be single or multiple, small and pale, or large and red and inflamed. They can be superficial or deeper in the dermis. Since almost any skin growth could be a mast cell tumor it is wise to have a needle biopsy or aspirate done on all skin growths.

These cancers can appear anywhere on the body, but tend to be found on the hind legs, lower abdomen, and around the groin area or penis (22). They may even show up on the legs.

Many families report that the size of the growth seems to change. One day it will be big, the next day it smaller. Touching or rubbing the growth may cause it to grow and become red and inflamed. Those changes are the result of histamine release by the cancer (27). Some dogs will itch in the area, too, because of the histamine release (2).

Rarely, dogs will show signs of stomach upset and gastric ulcers (such as vomiting or black stool). Again, this is a side effect of histamine release by the tumor (1).

Diagnosis

Diagnosing a mast cell tumor is very often done simply by a needle aspirate or biopsy. Mast cells have a characteristic appearance under the microscope. Mast cell tumors that are not well differentiated may need to have slides sent off to a pathologist. Your veterinarian may do some extra blood work looking for mast cells in the blood and may

Some cancer stories do have happy endings.

even recommend a bone marrow aspirate. Lymph nodes near the area may also be biopsied to look for any spread of the cancer.

While mast cell cancers rarely spread to the lungs, they can spread to the spleen or the liver. For that reason, your veterinarian may want to do ultrasound to look for any signs of metastasis to those organs (27).

Treatment

Treatment for mast cell tumors starts off with wide incision surgery. Remember, it is better to have a large incision the first time and get the tumor totally removed than to have to go back for a second surgery.

If there is any question about the surgery getting all the cancer, follow-up radiation is important. One study showed the dogs with radiation therapy had a two- to five-year survival rate of 96 percent (2).

Most dogs with mast cell tumors will also be on a variety of oral medications. Corticosteroids such as prednisone help to reduce some mast cell tumors and can certainly minimize the release and side effects of histamine. Prednisone may slow the growth of mast cell tumors as well as make your dog more comfortable (27). Antihistamine medications such as diphenhydramine (Benadryl®) are also used to reduce any histamine release effects. Medications to protect the stomach, such as cimetidine and ranitidine, may also be prescribed.

Deionized water has been injected into mast cell tumors with some favorable results, but is apparently quite painful (2).

Chemotherapy is not generally considered to be particularly helpful, but the drug l-asparaginase (33) may work for some cases.

Prognosis

Prognosis varies greatly with the stage of the mast cell tumor. Tumors that have well-differentiated cells are much more likely to be cured than tumors with very primitive cells. Boxers tend to have well-differentiated mast cell tumors and do quite well with treatment (1).

Location of the tumor seems to be a factor as well. Tumors on the legs respond better than tumors in the inguinal area and near the rectum (27).

Prevention and Care

These are common tumors and with some breed predispositions. Certainly, the best prevention is checking your dog for skin growths frequently and then having your veterinarian do needle aspirates on them.

Skin irritants may also be a factor in the development of mast cell tumors (1).

Breed Predispositions

Boxers and Boston Terriers are mentioned on every list of dogs with mast cell tumors (22, 27, 1, 2). Other breeds have been added as well— Golden Retrievers, Labrador Retrievers, Bullmastiffs, English Setters, Beagles, Schnauzers, Bulldogs, Bassets, and Weimaraners (27, 1, 2).

SUMMARY

- Oral cancers in dogs and cat are often associated with an owner who smokes.
- With feline meningioma (brain tumor), the prognosis is usually good if the surgery is successful.
- Canine mast cell tumors are the most common skin tumor in dogs.
- Over 80 percent of liver cancer has spread by the time it is diagnosed.
- Early detection greatly improves the odds of cure for these cancers.

5

Caring for Your Pet Who Has Cancer[1]

IN THIS CHAPTER

- Learn how to care for your pet who has cancer.
- Learn what's an emergency and what isn't.
- Learn how to get your pet to eat.
- Learn how to take your pet's temperature, and give medications.

Case Study

Jordie is officially known as CH Zephyre K-Two Just Do It UD HS AX OAJ. He is a handsome mahoghany-and-black, fluffy Belgian Tervuren. The alphabet soup around his name shows that he is both handsome and talented—competing in agility, obedience, and herding.

Jordie has always been active, happy, and healthy, though in the fall of 2003 he had a bad cough that led to pneumonia. So owner Julie reacted right away when he started coughing in the fall of 2004. Other than the cough, his only sign of illness was a slightly decreased appetite.

On examination, Jordie's vet could feel that his lymph nodes were enlarged a bit (impossible to see with that coat!). He also had a low fever.

---

1. (From Sources 39, 48, 49, 51, pages 211–215.)

Along with performance competitions, Jordie was an active therapy dog.

Because of Jordie's age (ten years), his veterinarian wanted to err on the side of caution and did a needle aspirate of one of the lymph nodes instead of simply assuming they were enlarged because of a respiratory infection.

On November 2, Julie got the news that Jordie had lymphoma. She responded immediately, using contacts to get him right into the oncology clinic at Colorado State. Julie elected to start right in with treatment, instead of going through staging, as she really wanted to get Jordie back on track.

Lymphoma is a cancer that normally responds to chemotherapy, so Jordie started on a chemotherapy protocol. His first treatment on November 3 was vincristine, which seemed to help, but on November 11 Jordie had a fever of 106 degrees and ended up in the ICU for two days. Chemotherapy reactions often take time to show up as the cell life cycles respond. A variety of drugs have since been tried, but with not much success.

Then on December 12, Jordie had an echocardiogram with showed some changes in his heart. This meant that Jordie could not safely go onto

Lymphoma can be treated with various methods.

the drug adriamycin unless he got the very expensive special heart protectant medication first. Julie elected to have a bone marrow aspirate as Jordie's next step in treatment. Luckily, his bone marrow showed very little change, so now Julie has time to investigate other possible drugs and protocols.

Jordie is anemic and tends to pant a bit, but is otherwise comfortable and happy and continues to eat well—including his special homemade meatloaf recipe (see below). Julie is supporting his immune system with acupuncture, salmon oil, "power" mushrooms, and the herb Artiminism.

Lymphoma is thought of as a very treatable cancer, but Jordie's case shows us that there are no simple answers to cances and that each individual has different responses to both the cancer and the treatments. Our fingers are crossed for him!

Jordie's Meatloaf

3 lb hamburger or ground turkey	1 can carrots
3 cups oatmeal or quick cook barley	1 can stewed tomatoes
	garlic
2–3 eggs	milk
1 can green beans	

Put oats in a large bowl and cover with milk. Soak until milk is
   absorbed (usually about 10 min)

Blend all the vegetables and their liquids.

Combine all ingredients and mix thoroughly. Place in a large
   cake pan and bake at 325 degrees until the liquid has evap-
   orated

Cool, cut, and serve.

Caring for your pet with cancer isn't simple, but there are things
you can do to make your life easier and your pet more comfortable.
In this chapter, we cover hospice care, that is, in-home care that you
can provide to help make your pet more comfortable.

IS THIS NORMAL OR SHOULD I PANIC?

Your dog or cat is going through a pretty stressful illness. Although
current cancer treatments take into account the patient's comfort and
quality of life, there can be some negative effects. Throughout this
book, we've been recommending that you communicate with your
oncologist and veterinarian—ask questions and get clarification on
what is normal and what is an emergency. As one friend with a dog
with cancer said to us, "I need to know what's normal and what
isn't—should I call the vet if my dog is peeing blue?"

   Your oncologist needs to tell you possible side effects of a particular treatment and what to watch out for. Some things, like nausea, hair loss, and lack of appetite, might be perfectly normal symptoms of the chemotherapy. Other times, a symptom may be something to discuss with your vet. Generally, anything out of the ordinary that you see should be reported to your vet or oncologist. While most pet don't have severe reactions to treatment, some do, and it's always better to be safe than sorry.

Although the following is not an exhaustive list, some symptoms that require a phone call and a possible trip to the vet or emergency room include the following:

- Fever (temperature 103F or more)
- Hypothermia (temperature 99F or lower)
- Shallow or thready pulse
- Sticky, dry lips; gray gums
- Dilated pupils or unresponsive pupils
- Weakness; inability to stand
- Blood in urine or feces
- Vomiting blood or black substances
- Projectile vomiting
- Dehydration
- Raspy breath; difficulty breathing
- Gray skin
- Shivering or shaking
- Seizures
- Extreme lack of appetite
- Unusual color in urine
- Loss of appetite for more than one day with cats; more than two days with dogs
- Collapse
- Disorientation

Diarrhea and vomiting may be signs of reactions to chemotherapy. Talk with your vet about how to control them so that they don't lead to more serious problems such as dehydration. Using a kaolin product will help control diarrhea (do not use the new Kaopectate® with bismuth salicylate on cats); ask your veterinarian for the proper dosage. Talk to your veterinarian and make sure you have medications on hand to help with nausea and vomiting and that you know the correct dose for your pet.

TAKING YOUR PET'S TEMPERATURE

Both dogs and cats have temperatures within the same normal range of 100–102.5 F. You can take your pet's temperature with a rectal thermometer (use the electronic kind—they're easier to use) or with an ear thermometer specially made for pets.

If you're taking your pet's temperature using a rectal thermometer, use petroleum jelly (Vaseline®) or K-Y Jelly ® to lubricate the end. Have someone hold your pet so that he is standing and gently insert the electronic thermometer into your pet's anus. Keep your pet standing while you wait. Usually an electronic thermometer will beep when ready, or you may time it to three minutes.

HOW TO GET YOUR PET TO EAT

One of the problems with cancer is that your pet may not feel well. Part of it is because of the cancer itself, but if she undergoes treatment, she may be sick from the treatment as well. Your vet may be able to help you with certain medications to stimulate your pet's appetite or offer certain prescription brands of pet food that are more palatable than regular commercial brands.

Now is not the time to withhold those tasty tidbits. Your pet needs all her strength to combat this disease. If she has a favorite food, start mixing it in with her regular pet food. (One friend I know fed Eukanuba® and Hagan Daz® to her dog with cancer when he wouldn't eat anything else). Are you spoiling her? Well, yes and no. She needs the nutrition to fight the cancer, and the only way she's going to get it is to eat.

Cats are especially problematic when it comes to not eating. A cat who doesn't eat can suffer from hepatic lipidosis—a life-threatening condition in cats—so never allow your cat to refuse food longer than twenty-four hours.

Here are some possible foods to try with your dog or cat:

- Lunchmeats
- Cooked ground beef, pork, turkey, or lamb
- Tuna fish
- Canned cat or dog food
- Ice cream
- Cheese
- Canned baby food (do not give any with onion powder)
- Canned mackerel
- Yogurt, plain
- A little garlic powder added to a favorite food

Sometimes warming the food in the microwave for a few seconds will make the food appetizing enough to eat. Some dogs and cats will lick the food off their cheeks or nose if you smear a little there. Cats may lick food off their paws if you rub some food on them. Usually once your cat or dog gets some taste of the food, it may stimulate their appetites enough to eat a bit more.

If your dog or cat simply won't eat, it's time for a trip to the vet. Your vet will be able to force-feed your dog or cat or may have to put him on an IV to get nutrition into him. Feeding tubes can also be placed to bypass a healing stomach or mouth incision.

CHECKING FOR DEHYDRATION

Dehydration can be a very serious condition in your pet. Dehydration can occur anytime, and if your pet is vomiting or has diarrhea, you must watch out for dehydration. You can tell if your pet is dehydrated by performing a skin-snap test. This is best done when your pet is not dehydrated, so that you can see what it looks like during normal circumstances. Most older pets have less elastic skin, and some breeds, like Shar peis, have skin folds that may alter the results.

Gently grasp the skin at the back of the neck, pull up, and release. In a healthy, young pet, the skin should snap back quickly. If the animal is severely dehydrated, the skin will stay there or slowly melt back. You can do the skin snap test on your pet's cheeks or feel his gums and mouth. If his gums are sticky or tacky, he's dehydrated.

Dehydration is serious. You can give your pet water or offer an unflavored pediatric electrolyte solution such as Pedialyte ® if he will drink. If he will not drink or if the dehydration isn't remedied, you will have to take him to your vet for fluid therapy. If dehydration keeps recurring or your pet has underlying kidney problems, ask your veterinarian to teach you how to safely give subcutaneous fluids at home.

MAKING YOUR PET COMFORTABLE

Because cancer is often a chronic disease, you should make your pet as comfortable as possible. After all, if your pet is comfortable, he'll feel better and that might help him recover faster from treatments and surgery.

One way to keep your pet comfortable is to provide a suitable bed. Since most pets who get cancer are middle-aged and older, many have arthritis or other conditions. You can find pet beds made with orthopedic foam. Some other pet beds are made to be waterbeds that help cushion sore joints. You can find these beds in pet supply catalogues and on the Internet.

If it's cold where you live, you might also want to consider a pet heating pad. Unlike human heating pads that can get too hot, pet heating pads are made for pets to lie down on and won't become too hot. In fact, some pet heating pads come with rheostats that enable you to adjust the temperature. These heating pads often come with a spring guard around the cord, but you should always keep the cord hidden. Keep the pad unplugged when you're unable to supervise.

Another difficulty your pet may face is getting in and out of cars or getting up on his favorite couch or perch. There are many pet ramps and pet staircases available for both cats and dogs. These ramps are great for dogs who need to climb in and out of cars and also for pets who can no longer climb up on the sofa or favorite perch.

But your pet's comfort shouldn't stop there. Look at where he eats, sleeps, and must relieve himself. Are there are staircases he must negotiate to get to these important places? Pain might keep your cat from getting to his litterbox down in the basement, or your dog with osteosarcoma may not be able to climb upstairs to get to his bed. Having everything accessible and on one floor will ease life for your pet.

KEEPING A PET LOG

One thing you can do to facilitate your pet's care is to get a notebook and keep a daily log of how your pet is doing. The log doesn't have to be fancy—just good enough to tell you the date, how your pet was feeling, how she ate, what care or medications she received, and whether anything special happened. That way, you can refer to the log when talking with your oncologist or veterinarian.

The pet log will keep you aware of any health changes attributable to cancer and treatment. By following the log, you'll have a day-by-day account of what has happened and you'll be able to give your veterinarian a better account of how the treatment is progressing. Saying "Shadow wasn't feeling that great last week" isn't as good as saying "May 23—After chemotherapy, Shadow didn't eat until I mixed beef juices in with her kibble. She had diarrhea and nausea." The log will help you remember things you might not always recall, such as how bouncy Rusty was after treatment or that he ate a half pint of ice cream.

GIVING YOUR PET MEDICATIONS

One other thing you'll have to do as your pet's caretaker is give your pet medicine. Most medicines come in pill form, but occasionally you may have to give medication in liquid form as well. Giving pills doesn't have to be difficult, but many owners have difficulty with it, so we're covering it here.

If the medication can be given with food, sometimes slipping the pill in a hot dog, a bit of peanut butter, or another tidbit works. If there's no danger in crushing the pill (some medications must be given whole), you can try crushing it and mixing it in with your pet's food.

However, if neither of these methods works (some dogs and cats are quite clever and will spit out the pill after eating the good stuff), you'll have to give the pill. Open your pet's mouth, place the pill on the back of the tongue, close his jaws, and tilt his head back. Gently stroke his throat until he swallows. (Blowing a tiny puff of air in your pet's nostril will also elicit a swallowing response.) "Pet pillers" that you can buy from pet supply houses help put the pill exactly where it needs to go if you're having trouble putting the pill on the back of the tongue.

To give your pet liquid medication, ask your veterinarian for an oral syringe (a syringe without the needle), and ask him to mark the dosage on the syringe. Gently pull on your pet's lower lip, and use the syringe to pour a little medication in it. Close your pet's mouth and tilt his head so he swallows. When he does, continue to administer the dose in this fashion until your pet has received the correct dosage.

If your pet needs chronic medications, talk to your veterinarian about getting the medication compounded into a flavored form, put in gel caps for easier pilling, or even into a gel form that might be absorbed through the skin. Compounding won't work with all medications, but can help with some.

Make sure you know *exactly* how to handle any chemotherapy drugs you may be giving your pet. You may need to wear gloves and carefully dispose of any wastes (including vomit, stool, and urine).

Sick cats often don't keep up with their grooming. Most of them greatly appreciate a quick daily going over with a slicker type brush for shorthair cats or a comb for longhair cats. Many dogs enjoy grooming as well, and both dogs and cats often respond to a massage.

This is a time to think about what your pet's favorite activities have been. If your cat prefers to snooze in a sunny window, make sure she can get to one. You can't always provide the sun, but at least have a soft bed or blanket there for her. If your dog loves long walks, make sure you continue that daily habit, even if you have to cut back drastically on the distance. And most of all, take the time to sit quietly with your pet, talking and sharing your time together.

SUMMARY

- Watch for unusual signs such as fever, dehydration, gray or sticky gums, seizures, or collapse, and seek veterinary attention immediately.
- Keep a log on your pet's health every day.
- You may need to entice your pet to eat. Use whatever your pet likes to eat.

6

Diagnosing Cancer

IN THIS CHAPTER

- Learn about the simple tests vets use to diagnose cancers.
- Learn about the high tech equipment used to diagnose cancer, such as the MRI, Ultrasound, CT or CAT scans, and scintigraphy.
- Learn how cancer is staged.
- Learn what diagnostic tools may be available in the near future.

D iagnosing cancer may be as simple as feeling a lump on your dog or as complicated as doing an MRI on your cat. Once you go beyond noticing something abnormal, you and your veterinarian will need to determine accurately not only whether the problem is cancer, but ideally what type of cancer. Think of cancer as a battle—you and your pet fighting against tumor cells. The first stage is to gather all the information you can.

Case Study

Tom Cat was a tiny kitten dumped off at Deb's parents' small farm. He was so tiny they weren't even sure at first if he was a boy or a girl! So until he grew a bit, his name went back and forth between Thomas and Thomasina.

Tom was a beautiful brown tiger with luxurious long fur when he grew up. He ended up so big he looked like a Maine Coon Cat. He lived in the barn, getting fed twice daily, receiving his health care and sleeping in the hayloft in summer and in a heated bed by the water pump in winter. Tom lived a life on "Easy Street," sleeping in the sun, doing a little hunting, staying plump. Other than needing occasional treatments for tapeworms (from his mouse hunting), he was healthy and happy.

When he turned about twelve years old, Tom moved into Deb's parents' house. He now went outside occasionally, but slept in sunny patches on the floor and enjoyed his "retirement." Then, at fourteen, Tom started to lose weight. He became more active and suddenly wanted to be fed four or more times a day instead of his usual two meals. A blood test showed very high thyroid levels, and he had a small nodule under his chin.

Tom went for surgery. Deb's parents weren't at all convinced they could give him daily medications and at that time there were very few radiation clinics. Luckily Tom was basically healthy otherwise, as his condition was caught early. Tom handled surgery like a trooper and had no complications.

Back to Massachusetts he went, to sleep in his sunny patches again and amuse grandchildren by playing gently. Three years later, Tom was found dead in his bed, curled up peacefully.

BLOOD AND URINE TESTS

Two of the simplest types of tests for cancer are blood tests and urine evaluations. Blood tests come in two basic types—the **CBC** or complete blood count and the blood chemistry or blood panel. The CBC looks at the red blood cells, the white blood cells, and the platelets. Your vet will check for anemia, infection, leukemias, and possible clotting problems.

The blood chemistry or blood panel checks out liver and kidney function, minerals such as sodium and calcium, and blood glucose (sugar). These tests indicate your pet's overall health and may show abnormalities that could point to a problem.

Most of the problems found on blood tests are what is called "**paraneoplastic syndromes.**" These are changes that can be thought of as side effects of cancer. The most frequent ones are anemia and **hypercalcemia.**

Anemia is a drop in the normal number of red blood cells. When this happens, the tissues do not get enough oxygen and other nutrients. Your pet may be weak and lethargic. If you check her gums, they may be pale. Anemia can be caused simply by the cancer cells draining nutrients or by cancer cells shoving out the normal cells in the bone marrow, spleen, and liver.

White blood cells, the cells that fight infection, increase with many cancers as your pet's body tries its best to fight off these abnormal cells. Many cancers leave pets open to secondary infections as well. Leukemias are cancers that cause an overgrowth of different white blood cells. This is one of the few cancer types that could be diagnosed with just a blood test.

Platelets are cells that help with blood clotting. Too few platelets may lead to bleeding problems. Some pets get **DIC (disseminated intravascular coagluation)** as a secondary effect of cancer. In this case, the body goes overboard with clotting. The blood components that control clotting get used up, and now your pet has bleeding problems.

Pets with cancer may show **hypoglycemia** or low blood sugar on tests. This can be the direct results of a cancer of the **pancreas** called an **insuloma** that makes extra insulin or from cancers of the liver. These pets are weak and may have seizures or even go into a coma.

Certainly, cancers of the liver or kidney may increase the enzymes associated with those organs or show changes in their normal working levels.

Increased calcium, called **hypercalcemia**, is one of the most common side effects of cancer. Lymphomas in particular seem to cause this problem. Pets with hypercalcemia drink more than usual, urinate more than usual, and may vomit and get dehydrated. Rarely, they have seizures, and the high level of calcium in the blood can slow the heart rate down. High blood calcium levels are not uncommon in young growing pets or pets with orthopedic trauma, but in most other pets this result would prompt further investigation.

For cats, an additional test for many possible cancers is a feline leukemia test. The retrovirus that causes feline leukemia also lowers your cat's natural immunity, making her more susceptible to a wide range of cancers. FIV (feline immunodeficiency virus) should be checked for the same reason.

Checking urine is another important step in intelligence gathering. Pets with cancer may show abnormal protein amounts in their urine or even cancerous cells such as from bladder tumors. These tests evaluate the kidney function of your pet and look for problems such as blood in the urine. Blood in the urine could mean a bladder infection, or it could mean that there are fragile tumor cells that are bleeding.

CT OR CAT SCAN

The jokes about "cat scans" abound, with cartoons showing a veterinarian waving a cat over a recumbent pet. Real **CT** or **CAT scan**s are much more complicated.

CT or CAT stands for computerized tomography or computerized axial tomography respectively (basically the same thing, so we will use CT from here on). The CT scanner uses many x-ray images to create a two-dimensional, cross-section image (7). The term "tomography" refers to the fact that thin slices of tissue are examined to avoid the overlap seen in traditional radiography (x-rays) (6).

Your pet is put into a tube with rotating x-rays of a very narrow beam. Despite their accuracy, CT scans should be avoided in pregnant pets, especially in the first trimester (7). The many images are computer analyzed to create the images your veterinarian will evaluate. Your pet must be sedated or anesthetized to minimize any movements that might distort the images.

The use of the computer can enhance details and emphasize changes seen. Sometimes contrast media are used to clearly mark normal and abnormal tissue lines as well.

CT is used for checking out joints, brain, and nasal tumors as well as evaluating the lungs carefully for any sign of metastases. CT scanning is also used for bone scans (1). They are very sensitive to any changes in bones, but then your veterinarian must carefully distinguish between changes from tumor versus changes caused by infection or arthritis. The sensitivity is useful for finding any metastases to the bones.

The use of CT scan is limited by availability as only large specialty practices or veterinary colleges tend to have the equipment. It does use ionizing radiation, so pregnant pets should avoid this. Sedation or anesthesia is required and it is expensive.

CYTOLOGY

Cytology is literally the study of cells. In the case of a cancer diagnosis, your vet examines cells to see if they are normal cells or tumor cells. The cells are checked under a microscope to look for any abnormal changes.

Cytology can be a very easy, quick, and economical way to make a diagnosis. Your veterinarian will put a needle into a growth and try to aspirate some cells that are then spread on a slide. Most pets handle this without even a flinch. For some growths, especially if they are ulcerated, your veterinarian may simply be able to put a slide against the tissue and collect cells that way.

Cells can also be looked at from fluid collected from the chest or abdomen or from lymph nodes in the area of a growth. Checking the cells from a urine collection may point out a bladder cancer. **Bone marrow** aspirates may be helpful too.

The drawback to cytology is that it can give a false negative, if only normal cells are collected on your sample. In this case, there actually is cancer, but the small sample did not pick up any of the "bad" cells. A normal sample may prove the growth is not a problem or that the cancer cells may have been missed. On the other hand, abnormal cells on the sample indicate a definite problem.

Your veterinarians will look at the cells under the microscope themselves, but if they are unsure of what they see, the slides may also be sent out to a **pathologist**. In both cases, the slides are checked to rule out possible inflammation and artifacts such as stain clumps. Then the cells are looked at for signs of malignancy. These include cells in an abnormal location for their cell type, an increased number of cells, cells of a wide variety of sizes and stages of growth, and lots of cells dividing (growing) (2). It is also important to try and determine the cell type to tell whether the growth is a primary tumor or a metastatic one.

Special staining techniques may be necessary to determine exactly what type of cells are present. Cytology can tell you if a cancer is present, give you an idea of what type of cancer it is, and may even help in planning treatment or knowing the prognosis. The knowledge is limited by the small sample size.

BIOPSY

A biopsy is a tissue sample taken to evaluate for any cancer or other abnormalities. This sample may be gathered by doing surgery or by using a special needle to take a "plug" of tissue.

Biopsies are generally classified in one of two ways. "Incisional" biopsies involve taking pieces of tissue from a growth to evaluate. In these cases, the vet is trying to determine exactly what type of cancer is present. This helps to decide on the definitive surgery or treatment plan. Your vet may be able to make prognosis statements or stage the cancer. A biopsy may help you, as the pet owner, make more informed decisions about treatment and even whether to treat or not.

An "excisional" biopsy is a sample from a surgery that totally (at least you hope totally) removes the cancer. For example, if your dog has a large, swollen spleen, it makes more sense to remove the spleen than to do a biopsy, losing time and possibly risking post-op **hemorrhage.** Doing the full surgery could even be a cure. An excisional biopsy may not be possible on some growths that will need radiation or chemotherapy follow-up.

When taking a biopsy, your veterinarian will try to get a margin with normal and abnormal tissue. That will help the pathologist accurately diagnose the cancer type. Most veterinarians do a biopsy assuming the growth is malignant, so don't be surprised if there is a good-sized incision. If the growth does come back malignant, the surgeon will try to remove any tissue that the biopsy might have contaminated with cancer cells, as well as the main growth.

Large needle tissue samples may be taken of the kidney or liver through the skin. It is best if these samples are taken with imaging guidance such as an ultrasound to guide the needle to the best possible site. Your pet should be tested for any clotting problems before this is done. Anesthesia or sedation may be required.

Stomach and intestinal samples may be taken by **endoscopy** (a thin scope passed down your pet's throat). This saves your pet from an abdominal incision, but it does give you a smaller sample size.

Risks associated with biopsies include post-op bleeding, anesthesia, and potentially "seeding" or spreading cancer cells. Still, the risks are usually minimal compared to the benefit of added knowledge in planning treatment and figuring out a prognosis.

MRI—MAGNETIC RESONANCE IMAGING

At first glance, **MRI** is one of those spooky technologies from the future. In this case, however, the future is now and is of major benefit to our pets.

How does MRI work? Many of us are familiar with the large tube that patients are slid into (new "open" models are gradually becoming available). This tube is essentially a large magnet and delivers radiofrequency pulses to your pet (no radiation). Subatomic particles called protons in the tissues react with the pulse and give off electromagnetic signals that "relax" at different rates depending on the tissue type. This signal intensity is recorded in a computer that generates an image for your veterinarian to examine (4).

Why is this diagnostic tool so helpful? You get very high contrast images showing excellent anatomic detail. The use of the computer can enhance images digitally, highlighting even tiny changes (7).

It works especially well when checking the central nervous system (brain and spinal cord) for tumors. Contrast dyes may be needed, but often the study can be done without the risk of using dye. Suspected nasal tumors and growths in the eye are also easier to evaluate with MRI. These evaluations may be used for initial diagnosis or to check out the invasiveness of a growth, plan a biopsy, and even plan treatments.

As mentioned, MRI is excellent for checking out brain masses and may be used more in the future for **musculoskeletal** problems in pets (as it is in people) (6).

Availability limits the use of MRI for our pets—only large centers such as big specialty practices or veterinary colleges have access to this technology; other limitations include the requirement for sedation or anesthesia and the cost. An MRI evaluation usually runs between $750 and $1500.

SCINTIGRAPHY

Scintigraphy is another advanced diagnostic technique. Radioactive isotopes are injected into your pet and a special "gamma camera" is used to detect where the radiation settles (2). The gamma radiation used here is less than the radiation used for traditional radiographs (x-rays), but precautions must still be taken until your pet has eliminated the radioactive materials.

As with MRI and CT scans, a computer is used to analyze the information gathered and generate digital images that can be enhanced for better detail. The radioactive drugs used include technetium–99m and pertechnetate (specifically for thyroid evaluations, as it is safer and less expensive) (2). The drugs used vary with the body system or area being evaluated. An example here would be phosphates used for studying bone turnover or pertechnetate for thyroid.

One of the pluses of scintigraphy is that it allows evaluation of **physiologic** (function) changes as well as anatomic changes. An increase in blood flow to a certain area or a change in blood flow patterns could hint at tumor spread. This capability could be especially useful for detecting cancers very early and for clearly outlining margins to help plan therapy (8).

Again, access to scintigraphy for pets is limited. Few facilities have the capabilities and the necessary equipment to do this safely. Cost is a factor as well.

RADIOGRAPHS/X-RAYS

Radiographs, more commonly called x-rays, use very low doses of radiation to evaluate tissues. The dosage used is much lower than that used for radiation treatments of cancer.

Rarely, top quality x-rays can be taken with a pet fully awake, but often pets require some sedation to achieve topnotch films. While anesthesia and sedation may concern you, remember that your pet's treatment plan may be decided by what is seen on these x-rays, so you certainly want the best possible quality. Don't be upset if you are not allowed to hold your pet for x-rays. Most state laws do not allow people in the same room where x-rays are being taken, and your veterinarian could risk losing her license if she allows you to stay with your pet.

X-rays are excellent for looking at bony tissues and tissues with air in them—such as lungs, intestines, and bladders. Virtually any pet with suspected cancer will have chest x-rays done. The lungs are one of the most common places for cancers to spread, and the presence of metastases can greatly influence your treatment plan. Most veterinarians take three views of the chest—one from each side plus one from top to bottom. Don't cut corners here—knowing about metastases is important!

To fully evaluate areas such as the intestines and bladder, your pet may need "contrast" studies. For those x-rays, dye or air or a combination of both are used to help define any abnormalities in the tissues being examined. A growth in the bladder that may not show up on a plain x-ray might be nicely outlined with a dye study.

While many veterinarians simply evaluate the films right in their office, some send films out or use telemedicine to have questionable areas checked out by a board-certified radiologist. Again, this is money well spent if your veterinarian has questions in her own mind.

ULTRASOUND

Ultrasound is another technology used to evaluate tissues. In this case, ultrasound waves are used instead of radiation. Many people are familiar with the ultrasound used for pregnant women—this is the same technique.

Ultrasound is excellent for evaluating soft tissues such as hearts, livers, spleens, and kidneys. It is not as good in general as x-rays for bones and lungs. One real plus of ultrasound is that it may be possible to differentiate problems on ultrasound. For example, an ultrasound may show that the growth in the liver is actually an abscess, not a tumor.

Ultrasound is considered to be excellent for evaluating hearts and can also pick up some functioning problems as well as structural changes. Pets on chemotherapy drugs that can affect the heart may need periodic ultrasound evaluations to be sure no heart damage has occurred.

Another good use for ultrasound in diagnosis is to help guide a needle biopsy. Your veterinarian can use the ultrasound picture, which is viewed on a screen, to help her put her needle right where the questionable tissue is.

For most ultrasound evaluations your pet will not need anesthesia, and you may be allowed to stay and help hold or comfort her. Ultrasound is not painful, but the gel can feel cool, and many pets do not like being held still and on their backs. To do a needle biopsy, some chemical restraint may be needed. It is important not to accidentally tear tissues, which could happen if your pet suddenly moves during a biopsy procedure.

STAGING A CANCER

Staging a cancer is part of the treatment plan of many cancers. At this point, you know your pet has cancer and you know what type of cancer. It is important now to determine the full extent of that cancer.

The World Health Organization offers a standard set of staging guidelines for solid tumors (31). These guidelines may be adjusted slightly for individual cancers, but the general stages are the same.

Three criteria are looked at: T for tumor size, N for whether or not the cancer has spread to local lymph nodes and other tissues, and M for spread or metastasis to tissues further away.

A dog with Stage I cancer has a localized growth, with no spread. Stage II still has the local growth, but now there is some spread to local lymph nodes. By Stage III, the local growth has invaded other local tissues fairly extensively and is into lymph nodes. Stage IV has all of the Stage III criteria plus spread to distant tissues. An example of Stage IV is a dog with breast cancer who has multiple glands involved, lymph nodes with cancer, and spread to the lungs.

Another staging system (showing how this can be adapted) can be seen with the staging guidelines for lymphosarcoma (3). These are not all solid tumors, so the criteria had to be adjusted. Stage I means that just one lymph node is involved. Stage II has multiple lymph nodes involved, but the tonsils are still cancer free. By Stage III, the pet has generalized lymph node involvement, with enlarged lymph nodes in many areas. In Stage IV, the liver, the spleen, or both, and possibly some of the lymph nodes as well have cancer. By Stage V, cancer is in the blood and bone marrow as well as other organs.

Staging is important to help your veterinary team and you decide on the best course of treatment for your pet. Obviously, a pet with Stage IV cancer needs either very aggressive treatment or perhaps simply hospice type comfort care. The age and health of your pet aside from the cancer are also important factors. Still, a thirteen-year-old dog with a Stage I cancer might warrant surgery that could be curative, while the same dog with a Stage IV cancer might be best off with palliative care only.

ON THE HORIZON IN DIAGNOSIS

Stromolysin is an enzyme associated with disease problems, including cancers. The gene that controls its production may even be actively involved in causing some cancers (17). A study with feline stromolysin showed that cats with levels of this enzyme, plus metastasis, had a poor prognosis compared to cats that did not have levels of this enzyme (17). What this tells us is that levels of this enzyme may be helpful to veterinarians and families as you plan treatment and care for your pet. We may also hope that some time in the future, genetic adjustments to the production of this enzyme might even be able to prevent or treat certain cancers.

Genetic markers for certain "cancer genes" are another hope for the future. These would not only aid in diagnosing cancers, but ideally could be used to screen and prevent cancers. Women with family histories of early onset breast cancer sometimes use this screening even now (30). And of course, the real hope for the future is that cancers with a genetic basis could be detected and fixed early in life by gene splicing or other genetic manipulations.

SUMMARY

- Simple blood tests and urine analysis can tell a veterinarian about certain types of cancer.
- Cytology, biopsies, and x-rays are simple ways to further diagnose a cancer or tumor.
- Veterinarians will sometimes need CAT or CT scans, MRIs, Ultrasound, and Scintigraphy to diagnose a type of cancer correctly.
- Staging a cancer is how veterinarians determine to what extent the cancer has spread.
- Genetic research offers new techniques on the horizon for diagnosing cancer.

Treatments for Cancer

IN THIS CHAPTER

- Learn what treatments are available for cancer.
- *Surgery*, *chemotherapy*, and *radiation* have often been considered the "big three" but are now joined with *hypothermia*, *cryosurgery*, and *photodynamic therapy*.
- Pain management is becoming very important in the treatment of cancer.

Advances in treating, and hopefully even curing, cancer are occurring every day. Refining new techniques, pushing the envelope on existing techniques, and exploring whole new areas such as **nanobiology**, immune therapies, and genetic manipulations make this an ever-changing area of study. Much of this initial research is done on animals and could have direct applications for our pets with cancer.

You and your veterinarian should thoroughly explore all treatment options. This should be done as soon as you have a diagnosis, because time is of the essence in successfully treating most cancers. Early detection and rapid, aggressive treatment lead to better prognoses. Look for studies that will treat pets for free or at greatly reduced cost if your pet fits the qualifications. Ask your vet or search the Internet for relevant studies.

Make sure you also consider the "support" treatments: providing excellent nutrition, exercise, and nursing care for your pet. Even if hospice care is your choice, you should research the best nutrition and pain medications. Your veterinarian should guide and advise you, but remember, YOU are your pet's best advocate!

Case Study

Phyllis Degioia knew something was wrong with her little Bichon mixed-breed, Fred. He had a small lump in his right anal sac. "He always had problems with expressing his anal sacs. I knew there was something going wrong when the lump doubled in size in one month," Phyllis says.

Some dogs lose hair during chemo. Fred is sporting a t-shirt to protect him from the elements and sunburn.

Fred went in for surgery and had the lump removed and biopsied. The lab results were not encouraging. It showed that Fred had adenocarcinoma of the apocrine gland of the anal sac—a very malignant tumor.

Fred was lucky—he lived close to the University of Wisconsin–Madison School of Veterinary Medicine where Fred was often used as a therapy dog. The vets there started Fred on chemotherapy and then radiation. The treatment was fairly aggressive: chemotherapy once every three weeks for four weeks. Radiation was to be given five times a week for three weeks.

"Fred had exceptionally bad luck during treatment," Phyllis says. "He had two bad reactions to the chemotherapy, which is very rare." Phyllis knew to keep watch for reactions and to bring Fred in as soon as possible. With the first reaction, Fred had bloody diarrhea and had a neutrophil (white blood cell) count of 182 (normal range is 3,000–165,000). The chemotherapy had caused bone marrow suppression in Fred, sending him to the emergency room. He spent two days in the ICU being treated with antibiotics.

Fred's second reaction to a different chemotherapy drug was very unusual. "After his third chemotherapy session, his neutrophil count went from normal to 260 in forty-eight hours," Phyllis said. "I knew something was wrong because Fred acted weird. He was shaking and became very clingy. When I felt him, he was hot—he had a fever of 104° F."

The second trip convinced Phyllis to stop chemotherapy treatment and continue with radiation treatment. Fred was rare also in that he lost his hair, and Phyllis had to knit him a sweater.

Fred never lost his appetite while receiving treatment, but that didn't stop Phyllis from worrying. She made a commitment never to leave Fred alone for any time—getting him pet sitters when she had to go out so that if something went wrong, she could get him to the emergency room as quickly as possible. She was very careful to watch for any unusual signs in the therapy and to report back to her veterinarian and oncologist.

Phyllis has a recommendation for anyone caring for a cancer patient. "Make sure you coordinate with your veterinarian and the vet school or

After his chemo treatments, Fred went back to being a therapy dog.

A handsome picture of Fred with his hair grown back.

oncologist. Make sure the specialist knows what your vet is doing and vice versa."

It's been a year since Fred's diagnosis. Was it worth it? Phyllis says without a doubt, it was. Fred is again his happy self: going for walks and working as a therapy dog.

SURGERY

Surgery is the first line in the battle against many cancers. In medicine, you hear surgeons say, "A chance to cut is a chance to cure." For some cancers that is true. The complete removal of cancerous tissue, which has not invaded local tissues or spread via the blood system or lymphatic system to other tissues, is a cure. Unfortunately, many cancers have already spread by the time they are diagnosed and surgery is done. Still, surgery to reduce the cancerous mass is a good thing, often making it easier for radiation or chemotherapy to fight the cancer cells as well.

The very first surgery done to remove a cancer has the best chance of a cure. The veterinary surgeon has the largest amount of healthy tissue surrounding the bad area, no scar tissue to deal with and no previous aggravation of the tumor cells. If a biopsy has been done to identify the tumor type, even the biopsy tract should be removed.

You might be surprised at how big the incision around the small growth your pet had is. Surgeons want wide "**clean tissue margins.**" That means a wide area of normal tissue around the growth, with no sign under the microscope of cancer cells invading the tissues. And remember, wounds heal side to side, not end to end! A six-inch-long wound will heal as fast as a one-inch-long wound. A pet with mammary (breast) cancer may have incisions that run the length of her body, but better a long incision than to leave any cancerous tissue behind. With cats in particular, veterinarians tend to want very wide margins, as so many feline tumors are malignant.

Any lymph nodes nearby that are enlarged will be removed as well. They could be sources of cancer cells to "seed" elsewhere.

Before any surgery, your pet's veterinarian will run blood tests and take radiographs (x-rays) to check the overall health of your pet. The blood tests will look for anemia, liver or kidney damage, and any important changes in blood minerals. The x-rays will be looking for any detectable spread of the cancer—particularly to the lungs or liver. Unfortunately, microscopic spread is not detectable by x-rays.

If there are signs that the cancer has already spread from the initial growth, more research will be needed to determine if it makes sense to put your pet through surgery. If she has a cancer that responds well to radiation or chemotherapy, it may still make sense to remove the primary mass and then treat the others.

This is one of those areas where the assistance and input of a veterinary **oncologist**, a specialist in animals with cancer, is vital. These veterinarians know from experience and training how certain cancers behave and the best ways to treat them. It may make sense, for example, to put radioactive beads into the surgery site. Sometimes it is best to do some pre-operative radiation or chemotherapy to shrink the tumor down to a reasonable size for surgery.

Surgery may be done for a number of reasons. To totally remove all cancer and cure your pet is an ideal goal but not always realistic. Some brain tumors or other tumors intertwined in healthy tissue cannot be safely removed. If your pet already has widespread metastases, it may not make sense to spend much of her remaining lifetime trying to recover from a surgery.

In some cases, surgery is done for palliative reasons. Removing the spleen from a dog with hemangiosarcoma is unlikely to cure that dog. It may, however, gain some quality-life time for that pet and prevent the rupture of tumors and severe internal bleeding. Palliative surgery may also be done to relieve pain in pets with bone cancer or ocular tumors that have caused glaucoma.

Debulking is when surgery is done to reduce a large tumor in the hope of making radiation, cryotherapy, or chemotherapy more effective (basically, fewer cells to kill). If surgery is to be combined with chemotherapy, the chemotherapy may not start until seven to ten days post-op to reduce the chances of chemotherapy drugs interfering with the wound healing. The same with radiation—depending on the type of cancer, treatment may start right after surgery (even during surgery) or it may wait until the wound is healed.

Preventive surgeries include spaying and neutering for pets with hormone-responsive cancers.

Rarely, surgery may be done to treat a metastatic cancer, such as a single lung mass. This is not common but might be done.

Many new surgical techniques can be used to perform miraculous treatments. Limb-sparing surgeries can leave a giant breed dog with osteosarcoma a chance to walk better for his remaining time. Removing a jaw sounds drastic to us, but many pets adapt quite well. Deb met a Golden Retriever who had two extra years of life after surgery to remove her upper jaw on one side, and she could even still sniff her way around a track! Plastic surgery can help reduce the scarring after a large tumor has been removed. Brain tumors can sometimes be treated with surgery, leaving your pet with a dramatic improvement.

CRYOSURGERY

Cryosurgery is a treatment technique that uses cold to kill off cancer cells. Tissues undergo cycles of freezing and thawing that cause the cells to die. Obviously, very cold temperatures must be used for this to work.

There are two versions of cryosurgery—one uses liquid nitrogen and the other uses nitrous oxide. These may be sprayed over tissues or put through probes (1).

Cryosurgery is used primarily for superficial tumors such as those on eyelids or the skin, in the mouth, and around the anus. It should be used very carefully around bones. This technique may also be used to **debulk,** or reduce in size, a large tumor so that other treatments are more effective. Cryosurgery is not recommended for use on mast cell tumors, osteosarcomas, nasal tumors (as it might damage too much normal tissue), or tumors that go all the way around the anus (as it might damage important nerve tissue).

Pets having cryosurgery may simply need a local anesthetic for small growths. General anesthesia is needed for larger growths or growths in very sensitive areas such as around the eye.

Your pet may have some mild discomfort, but it is not bad. (Deb says that with confidence as her son had numerous warts—actually small, virus-caused cancers—removed via liquid nitrogen and he had no anesthesia of any kind.) The tissues that have been frozen and thawed will swell a bit and turn dark. They may ooze and even look infected before they scab and then fall off. Your dog or cat should not be allowed to rub or lick the area, so your pet may need an Elizabethan collar for a short time.

The pluses to cryosurgery are that it is fast, easy, and safe with minimal bleeding to worry about. Drawbacks are the need for special equipment—the probes, storage for the nitrogen—and the lack of margins when you treat. You hope that you are getting all the cancer but sometimes it is hard to tell. Repeat treatments or follow-ups with other treatments may be needed.

HYPERTHERMIA

The opposite treatment option from cryosurgery is **hyperthermia.** This treatment version uses heat to damage and kill cancer cells. This is almost always done with chemotherapy and/or radiation.

Pets are treated with a handheld radiofrequency device or microwave (3). Tumors tend to have abnormal **vasculature** (blood vessels), which makes them more susceptible to heat damage (1). The hyperthermia also makes the tissues more sensitive to radiation and to the effects of certain chemotherapy drugs such as cisplatin and doxorubicin. Your veterinarian may be able to reduce the dose of these drugs if chemotherapy is combined with hyperthermia.

Hyperthermia treatment is not that common. Many clinics do not have facilities and equipment to do this. This technique works best on growths less than one centimeter in size and for soft tissue sarcomas (1).

Hyperthermia-treated areas can be quite painful post-op, so your pet will definitely need pain medications.

PHOTODYNAMIC THERAPY

Photodynamic therapy is another relatively new treatment technique. This technique uses light-sensitive substances combined with laser to damage cells.

For this treatment, your pet is given an injection of one of the special substances that are very sensitive to certain light waves. The exact substance can be chosen to have an affinity for certain types of tissues and many preferentially go to tumor sites (1).

Once the substance is in the tissues, light, via a laser with infrared wavelengths, is shone on the area. This creates toxic forms of oxygen, called free radicals, which then kill the cells where the substance is (2). Special fiber optic light sources can be used to pinpoint exactly where the light will go. General anesthesia is usually required.

The photodynamic therapy won't work on tumors deeper than two centimeters (3). This treatment has been used successfully on basal and squamous cell sarcomas, as well as transitional cell carcinomas of the bladder (2). While it may not totally remove some tumors it can be palliative and keep your pet comfortable for an added time.

This is not a common technique at this time, but may become more widely used in the future. A major plus is that the damage to normal tissues is minimal; it is selective for the cancer cells. Drawbacks are the need for special equipment and the expense. The substances injected to elicit photosensitivity will cause at least minor sun sensitivity for your pet's skin and eyes of for up to six weeks (3). This means you must take precautions to keep your pet out of bright sunlight.

RADIATION THERAPY

Radiation therapy uses radiation to treat cancer by killing the cancer cells with radiation and/or stopping the cells from dividing and reproducing. It can be used to try to cure a cancer but also for palliative care to relieve pain. The dosages of radiation used are much higher than those used for diagnostic x-rays.

The machines used for radiation therapy have special collimators that force the radiation into a very narrow beam. That way the damage to normal tissues around the cancer is minimized.

Before your pet is selected for radiation therapy, a full workup needs to be done. First, your veterinarians will need to know exactly what type of cancer they are fighting and whether that cancer will even respond to radiation therapy. Then, they will try to get the best possible idea of exactly where the tumor is, if it has invaded other areas, if there are any metastases, and so on. A CT scan or MRI may be important.

A customized radiation treatment plan will be drawn up showing exactly where to aim the beam and what dose to use and how often, and the sites will be marked right on your pet (11). Give your pet a thorough bath and any grooming trims you normally do before you start treatment. Once the special markers are put on your pet's skin so that the x-rays can be aimed exactly where they need to go, your pet shouldn't be bathed.

Many veterinarians recommend doing any necessary tooth cleaning or dental work before you start radiation therapy as well (11). That way, there are no unexpected areas of irritation or infection to interfere with treatment.

Once all of that information is gathered, it is important to know whether your pet can handle repeated, even though short, anesthesias. General anesthesia is important as your pet must be perfectly still so the radiation beams can be lined up exactly on the cancer. Radiation therapy may be combined with surgery or chemotherapy (and when combined with chemotherapy, you might be able to reduce the dosage of the chemo medications).

Radiation therapy is expensive. A short course of palliative radiation may run around $2,000 or more, while a full attempted cure series of treatments could be $3,500 to $4,500 or more. That cost estimate is just for the radiation treatment—the workups and diagnostics are extra (10).

Most pets are treated on an outpatient basis for five days of the week for a definitive treatment. This therapy is undertaken with the expectation that your pet will live at least a year after treatment. Rarely, a pet will have radiation therapy before any surgery is done on the cancer. Radioactive pellets may even be put into the surgery site in some cases. Normally, though, radiation follows the surgery.

You need to realize that your pet will show some acute side effects from radiation therapy. These may take three to six weeks to resolve and won't show up immediately. Most pets get worse about seven to ten days after treatments end, then gradually improve (11).

What side effects might you see? This will depend partly on the area receiving treatment. Acute side effects usually respond well and disappear a few weeks after treatment ends. Most pets show some fatigue (understandably). Pets who have had their abdomens treated may have nausea and some vomiting. Most pets will lose the hair over the site of the radiation beam focus and the hair either may not grow back or may grow back a different color.

Mucosal tissues like those around the mouth may be dry and cracked. Pets with oral treatment may drool or have very bad breath. Eyes may be dry and crusty, bladder or **colon** irritation is possible, and a cough from **tracheal** irritation may occur. Pets whose paws have been in the radiation beam may slough the bottom of the pads or lose their toenails or claws. Antibiotics, prednisone, and topical ointments may be important to help your pet heal quickly.

Long-term or late side effects are also possible. Tissues that do not normally divide and renew themselves are at greatest risk of damage. These are not common but may occur. Connective tissues and vasculature are at greatest risk. Effects you might see include nonhealing skin ulcers, muscle contractures, strictures of the gastrointestinal tract, cataracts, and hair color changes. In people, long-term effects could include inducing other cancers, but most pets do not experience that due to shorter life spans.

What cancers are possible candidates for radiation therapy? Nasal tumors have a moderate response with 50 percent of dogs surviving for a year after treatment. Oral squamous cell tumors in dogs do well—alone or in combination with surgery, as do feline nasal squamous cell carcinomas. Melanomas of the jaw seem to do about the same whether treated with surgery (removing half of the jaw) or radiation. Some of the best success rates come from soft tissue sarcomas. Dogs may survive up to three years after a radiation therapy series. Cats with vaccine-induced sarcomas may do well for 1.5 to 2.6 years after surgery combined with radiation or radiation and chemotherapy (12). Bone tumors are often radiated for pain relief—survival time beyond seventy to ninety days is not improved but dogs are much more comfortable after one to two weeks of treatment (10).

CHEMOTHERAPY

Simply put, chemotherapy is the use of medications to fight and kill cancer cells. This therapy is used most often for cancers that have already spread and cancers that are in blood or lymphoid tissues. Chemotherapy may be used alone or it may be used in combination with other cancer treatments. Chemotherapy may also be used to induce a remission in your pet's cancer or to maintain a remission. Different drugs and different dosing schedules and dosages may be used (1).

More than any other cancer therapy, chemotherapy seems to bring up tales of suffering and discomfort. Chemotherapy in pets is often different from chemotherapy in people. In people, high doses are used with a much higher risk of side effects, as doctors are hoping for a very long-term remission. For example, it makes sense to risk making you extremely ill for six months to gain twenty years of life. If your pet is already twelve years old, with a normal life expectancy of fifteen years, six months of risk for severe side effects isn't all that great. It makes more sense to use a lower dosage and aim for four or five cancer-free years. Also, our pets seem to handle many side effects better than we do—perhaps because they don't have the extra mental worry!

Chemotherapy can be quite expensive, but there are more generic options now. You may be able to arrange for your own veterinarian to administer the treatments so you don't need to have the added expense of travel to a specialty facility (see Fang's Case Study in chapter 3). Expect that your pet may have some extra expenses for possible side effects from the treatments, maybe even some hospitalization.

Whether or not your pet needs chemotherapy will depend on the exact type of cancer she has and possibly also the stage. A cancer that is a single mass and is totally removed with surgery may not need follow-up chemotherapy. Any cancer with signs of metastasis will probably have chemotherapy among the treatment options. And virtually all lymphomas and leukemias use chemotherapy as their primary therapies.

Your veterinarian will want to work up your pet thoroughly, as the exact chemotherapy drugs used may depend on any underlying health conditions your pet already has. For example, dogs with heart conditions may not get the drug doxorubicin (adriamycin) as part of their treatment. Background blood work will be done, both to check for any underlying problems and to establish a baseline to check future blood tests against. X-rays and/or ultrasound exams may be done to establish whether or not there are metastases already. Sadly, if your pet has evidence of extensive spread of her cancer already, with a poor prognosis even with treatment, you may elect to go for "comfort care" and make her as comfortable as she can be for the rest of her time.

Chemotherapy can be given in a variety of ways. Many chemo drugs are given intravenously through a catheter carefully inserted into one of your pet's veins. Some of these drugs must be given slowly over time and mixed with fluids to prevent damage to the veins. Do not be surprised if your veterinarian says your pet must be hospitalized for a few hours for treatment. A few drugs can be given by injection under the skin, and some are given as oral pills. It is important to remember that these are toxic drugs—after all, their job is to kill cells! These medications affect people as well as pets, so you may need to wear gloves to handle pills and possibly even take special precautions with your pet's urine or stool.

Catheters are important for giving many chemotherapy drugs, because these drugs can be very caustic and do extensive tissue damage if they get outside of a vein. An experienced veterinary technician or your veterinarian will always carefully place the catheters and then verify that there is no leakage (3).

The ideal chemo drug would kill only cancer cells, without harming any normal cells and without causing any side effects. So far, that miracle drug has not been found. Because chemo drugs ideally go for rapidly dividing cells, your pet's normal intestinal cells and blood cells are at risk. This is why blood counts are often done right before any chemotherapy treatments. If your pet's counts are too low, a treatment may be postponed. Anemia contributes to overall weakness, and low counts of the white blood cells that fight infection could leave your pet vulnerable to deadly bacteria or viruses.

Different chemotherapy drugs work at different stages of cell reproduction or kill cells in other ways. For this reason, some of the best successes using chemotherapy come from using a combination of drugs—called a protocol. You will hear experienced owners of pets with cancer discussing CHOP or MOPP—all of them acronyms using the first letter of different chemotherapy drugs. P is almost always present—for prednisone, which is a corticosteroid that has many uses, not just cancer fighting.

It has been established that the best way to attack cancers with chemotherapy is to go at them with all guns blazing. Starting right off with an aggressive protocol gives the best chance for a fast and long remission. Lower dosages or using fewer drugs may lead to the development of resistance among the cancer cells—just like bacteria becoming resistant to certain antibiotics. If your pet shows a drastic reaction to a certain drug, the protocol can be adjusted. If your pet has a nice long remission, but then the cancer returns, the same protocol may be tried again, or a different one used to try to avoid resistance.

Chemotherapy protocols have set time schedules for dosing. The schedule takes into account the time needed for cell replication cycles and makes sure that the drugs are not going to interfere with each other. Dosages for chemotherapy drugs are almost always determined by size. This does not mean a dose per pound like most medications, but rather the dose is based on body surface area—given in meters squared or m^2 (3). Your veterinarian will have a chart that converts your pet's weight to meters squared. If your pet loses weight, adjustments will be made.

Along with the correct dose and the overall timing schedule, the exact time of day your pet receives her treatment may be important too. **Chronobiology** looks at the daily, weekly, and monthly rhythms of your pet's body. For example, studies have shown that the liver gets its maximum blood flow of the day at 8 A.M. This could influence your treatment time if the drug being used gets removed by the liver or if it might be toxic to the liver. Intestinal cells do their maximum DNA synthesis between 5 and 9 A.M., so morning might not be the best time for a medication that has gastrointestinal side effects, but it could be the best time for treating an intestinal cancer. Bone marrow has most DNA synthesis between 7 A.M. and 4 P.M., so again, that timing can be taken into consideration when scheduling your pet's chemotherapy appointments. Another study showed that there were fewer toxic side effects when cisplatin was given in the afternoon and doxorubicin was given in the morning (2).

You can expect that a pet on chemotherapy will be taking other medications as well. These may include medications for vomiting or diarrhea, antibiotics to combat any infections, and vitamins or supplements to help keep your pet's normal cells healthy and strong. Special medications to increase the production of blood cells may also be used. Always discuss any supplements with your veterinarian. Some chemotherapy drugs work by oxidating cancer cells to kill them. Giving antioxidant supplements might counteract the effects of those drugs (21).

The most common side effects of chemotherapy include vomiting, loss of appetite, and damage to blood cells. Vomiting, sometimes with diarrhea, is a result of the effects of these drugs on the rapidly dividing and growing cells of the intestinal tract. Remember that your dog could be vomiting up some of the drug if you recently gave her a chemotherapy pill. Clean up thoroughly and with care!

If your pet starts to vomit after a treatment, contact your veterinarian. Your veterinarian will discuss safe antiemetics to use—possibly over-the-counter meds like Pepto Bismol®, the spice ginger, or possibly a prescription medication such as Reglan®. The important thing is to stop the nausea. Your veterinarian will also have you check for dehydration—seeing if the gums are moist and if your pet's skin snaps back quickly into place after you "tent it up." If needed, your pet may receive extra fluids, either under the skin or via an intravenous catheter.

Diarrhea can be another effect of the chemotherapy drugs on those intestinal cells. Again, there may be potent drug remnants in that stool, so clean up thoroughly and carefully. This is another case where it is also possible for your pet to become dehydrated. Do the skin test, check the gums, and call your veterinarian if needed. You should also check with her about medications to help control the diarrhea and any secondary infections. Adding some fiber to the diet may help slow down the flow as well.

Not eating well may be simply a side effect of the nausea. It is important to try and keep your pet's general health up, as she is dealing with both fighting the cancer herself and handling side effects of her treatments. Ideally your pet is on a very good diet, possibly one of the "cancer diets" shown to help pets with this problem. However, if she is not eating, this is the time to resort to beloved goodies, unusual snacks, and so on. For some reason, many pets with cancer love ice cream—vanilla being a top flavor. Check with your veterinarian in case your pet has other health problems that could be exacerbated by some of these treats, but if not, go for it.

Arginine may be added to diets to help slow tumor growth and spread (21). If you are home cooking for your pet, discuss adding this to her diet with your veterinarian. Remember that cancer diets should be high in protein and fat, with fewer carbohydrates. There are both prescription versions of this diet and homemade recipes (21).

A more immediately serious side effect can be an allergic reaction to the drug used. If you notice your pet getting a swollen muzzle or having difficulty breathing, call your veterinarian right away and head to the clinic. Cisplatin is rarely used in feline chemo protocols for this reason. This medication may then have to be dropped from the protocol or the dosage drastically reduced.

Fevers may occur as a result of the medication itself or secondary to the destruction of cancer cells. Either way, a high fever can wipe out your pet. Learn how to take your pet's temperature, and have medications on hand to give if you need to. Any temperature over 103 degrees rates a call to your veterinarian for a plan of action.

Sadly, your pet will become accustomed to many blood tests over the course of chemotherapy. The blood cells (both red and white) have fairly short life spans and are constantly being replaced. Anemia is not as common as low white blood cell counts, but may require supplements and medications to increase the red cell count. A low white blood cell count means that your pet is more vulnerable to infections. A very low count may mean postponing a treatment so your pet's body can recover a bit. Antibiotics may be prescribed at this time to help fight off any infections.

Hair loss is devastating to people, but pets don't seem to mind it. Cats may feel the loss of whiskers more than dogs, but many pets barely seem to lose any hair at all. Dogs such as Poodles, Old English Sheepdogs, and Schnauzers who have different hair growth cycles may show hair loss more than others (3). With long-term chemotherapy, many dogs will lose their long, outer guard hairs. If areas need to be shaved for catheters and treatments, hair may be slow to grow back or could grow back another color. Areas of skin under where the hair has been shaved may change color as well. Deb's Wiley had a skin change color from pinkish to black where his intravenous catheters had been. Sun lotion may help on these areas. Remember, if your pet has suffered from hair loss or coat thinning, she may need a coat or sweater to go out in bad weather.

Cardiac effects of some chemotherapy drugs may be life threatening. Doxorubicin (adriamycin®) is a drug that can cause serious damage to your pet's heart. A "lifetime maximum dose" for this medication has been established, and pets rarely receive more than that during their course of treatment. Routine EKGs and echocardiograms will be done to watch for any signs of cardiomyopathy. A drug called ICRF 187 may minimize the cardiac effects of doxorubicin and can be given as a pretreatment (3).

A fairly common complication of treatment with the chemotherapy drug cyclophosphamide is bloody urine (hemorrhagic cystitis). The metabolites of this drug cause a sterile irritation of the bladder tissue if left in contact for very long. Pets receiving this drug will often get additional fluids to flush the bladder and dilute the metabolites. Morning treatments to allow your pet all day to drink and urinate will help. Pets receiving prednisone as well may get that medication at the same time, as prednisone tends to stimulate extra drinking and frequent urinating (3). This can be a frightening side effect but is not usually serious.

There are a few chemotherapy drugs that can cause neurological signs. This could mean disorientation or even seizures. The drug 5-flourouracil is not used in cats because of this side effect (3).

Realize that most of these side effects are not life threatening. It is important to let your veterinarian know about any of these, though, so dosages can be adjusted or drugs changed if necessary.

MELPHALAN

Melphalan is the short name for L-PAM, L-Phenylalanine mustard, and L-Sarcolysin. We only need to know that this is one of the newer chemotherapy drugs being used in pets today.

Melphalan was derived from the terrible toxins used in World War I such as nitrogen mustard gas. It is in the same "family" of drugs as cyclophosphamide. The targets are actively reproducing and growing cells, which includes most tumor cells.

As with all chemotherapy drugs, we need to remember that the job of melphalan is to kill cells. The goal is to have a chemotherapy drug that will only and always kill just cancer cells.

This medication can be given orally or by intravenous injection. While not approved for use in pets by the FDA, melphalan has been used primarily to treat pets with blood origin cancers like leukemias and myelomas. In people it has had much more widespread trials—including for breast cancer, ovarian cancer, and at high doses to wipe out bone marrow in preparation for bone marrow transplants (20)—clearly a serious drug!

Melphalan should be used very carefully in pets with kidney problems and pets whose bone marrow is already struggling to keep up with the demands of fighting cancer. Some pets may show allergic reactions, so your pet should be observed carefully after any treatment—don't zip by the vet's office, get your pet treated, and zip home to leave her while you head off to a long day at work! Have someone available to watch your pet for several hours, even if it means spending the day at the clinic.

A few pets will have stomach upsets, and some will suffer from bone marrow damage—usually noted by low platelet counts, so bleeding problems are a possibility, and low white cell counts, so infections are more likely. Breathing problems have been seen in people.

Pets with kidney failure or who have been through radiation treatment should not receive melphalan unless it is clearly the best option.

All of this makes melphalan sound very toxic and dangerous, which it is. However, its success rate with myeloma is quite good, with some dogs surviving up to 540 days (20)!

PAIN MANAGEMENT

One of the most important parts of cancer treatment is trying to keep your pet pain free. Not only is that much kinder and more humane, but animals who are pain free heal better and faster, eat better, and can put extra effort into fighting their cancer.

With our pets, we often rely on their behavior to tell us if they are in pain (1). Dogs who pant abnormally, cats who lie very still and quietly for long periods of time, or almost any change in behavior could be an indication of pain. Limping is a simple sign to see, but things like avoiding chewing or lying on the floor instead of climbing up on the couch could be indications of pain somewhere. Sometimes pets who have always been tolerant suddenly snap or turn their heads quickly when touched in sensitive areas.

It is important to remember that our pets often try to hide signs of pain. They can be stoic, but such behavior is also adaptive. An animal in the wild who shows any sign of weakness may be attacked by her own pack or driven off, to prevent predators from being attracted to the group. Harsh, but important for survival of the species.

Pain is usually described in two or three ways. "Somatic" pain is pain in bones and muscles. This might be post-op pain and is usually localized. "Visceral" pain arises from pressure on organs by growing tumors. This pain may be accompanied by nausea. Pain may also be labeled as "acute" or "chronic." Acute pain would fit a broken leg, which will heal and be nonpainful eventually. An example of chronic pain would be degenerative arthritis—this won't ever totally go away but can be managed.

Research has shown that it is best if pain medications are given early—even before surgery, for example, instead of waiting until after (3). So more veterinarians are incorporating pain treatment right into the basic care plan for pets with cancer.

As mentioned, surgery and radiation can be used themselves for palliative care. Radiation seems to be particularly helpful for bone pain and, of course, surgery to remove a cancerous limb would relieve pain once the surgical site healed. Some veterinarians now start epidurals and local nerve blocks while your pet is still anesthetized, to provide a pain-free start to healing (2).

Acupuncture is a procedure that is gaining many proponents for pain management in pets (27). Acupuncture has virtually no side effects and can be combined with many medications for a cumulative effect. Multimodal pain therapy (using a variety of techniques and medications) is very effective and may provide the best pain relief (2).

A wide variety of pain medications is available for pets, especially dogs. Cats metabolize many drugs differently than dogs or people because of the lack of a certain liver enzyme. For that reason, they can't safely be given many pain medications.

It is common to start off with fairly mild pain medications (except immediately post-op), then build up to stronger drugs as needed. Piroxicam, metacam, and carprofen are all used, as well as aspirin. Aspirin can be used in cats, but only at a greatly reduced dosage and frequency. Always consult your veterinarian before using ANY pain medications. You need to be sure the pain medications won't interfere with any other drugs your pet may be getting. Also, if your pet has liver or kidney problems, it is best to avoid certain drugs.

Stronger medications include the opioid drugs. Butorphanol is an excellent pain medication and can be given by injection. Fentanyl patches (small patches of medication applied to shaved areas of skin) are very popular (3). These patches gradually give off a steady dose of pain medication without your pet having to be bothered. Always carefully follow directions on using these patches—they need to be handled carefully and you don't want your pet licking them or chewing on them.

There are some herbs that are considered to be pain medications. These include dandelion (weak, but safe for cats) and feverfew. The enzyme papain and the spice turmeric have also been used as pain medications (21).

Slightly off the beaten path of most veterinary care is the use of magnets. These are reputed to increase blood flow to specific areas and may help with some cancer pain (22).

Nursing care is an often overlooked aspect of pain management as well. Keeping your pet comfortable—on soft warm beds or on cool, comfortable surfaces—is helpful. Make sure that food and water are at temperatures that your pet prefers. Gentle massages and the use of TTouch® can be very important. Sometimes even just quiet companionship helps to settle an uncomfortable pet.

SUMMARY

- Surgery is often the first treatment of cancer to remove the entire cancer.
- Cryosurgery is used to remove tumors through freezing the cells and thereby killing them.
- Hyperthermia uses heat to kill off cancer cells.
- Photodynamic therapy uses light-sensitive substances and lasers to destroy tumors.
- Radiation therapy is used to kill cancers in a localized area with high dosages of radiation.
- Chemotherapy uses medication to kill off cancer cells that may have spread to other parts of the pet's body.
- Melphalan is a new chemotherapy drug that has a high success rate in dogs for myeloma.
- There are various ways to manage pain in your pet. These include medications but can also include surgery and radiation. Veterinarians are also using holistic therapies such as acupuncture and massage to help mitigate pain.

8

New Techniques and Cancer Studies[1]

IN THIS CHAPTER

- Learn about up-and-coming techniques for treating cancer.
- Learn how veterinarians are trying not just to cure cancer but also to improve the quality of life in their patients.
- Learn what new techniques are available to help with diagnosing cancer.

Imagine genetically engineered viruses specially concocted to wipe out cancer. Imagine being able to give medication to a dog or cat that attacks the cancer and leaves the good cells. Imagine looking deep within your dog's or cat's body and with a three-dimensional image to determine whether the tumor in the liver is benign or malignant. Imagine shutting down cancer cells with a simple flip of a switch in the cells. Imagine supercharging the animal's immune system to recognize and fight off the cancer. Farfetched, you say?

---

1. (From Sources 39, 41, 42, 43, 44, 55, 56, pages 211–215.)

The stuff in this chapter borders on science fiction, but it's not. It's happening now. Right now in various cancer studies, veterinary oncologists and researchers are doing those things and more. They're working toward making cancer, if not a thing of the past, then at least a condition you and your veterinarian can knock back when it shows up again.

This is the kind of thing we all dream of—and yet this isn't a fantasy. Hundreds of researchers are working toward the day when pet owners hear the word "cancer" and shrug it off because it doesn't mean their pets will die. Let's look at some of the new treatments on the horizon.

CANCER VACCINES

One particularly promising method to attack cancer comes from genetic research. Veterinarians are developing ways to kick the animal's immune system into high gear with the use of cancer vaccines.

One leading edge technology comes from Memorial Sloan-Kettering in conjunction with the Donaldson-Atwood Cancer Clinic at the Animal Medical Center in New York. Dr. Philip Bergman, DVM, head of the Donaldson-Atwood Cancer Center and diplomate of ACVIM is leading research there on vaccinations against certain forms of cancer.

The technology makes use of lessons learned in genetic research and molecular technology. Cancer is insidious because the body often doesn't recognize the cancer cells as being foreign, so the body's immune system doesn't attack them. The vaccine is made from DNA that appears in another host such as mice or even humans. Because the DNA is from a foreign host, the dog's immune system attacks the vaccine and then "recognizes" the cancer cells as being foreign and attacks the cancer cells. Currently, studies are ongoing, but show significant progress and at this time show no apparent side effects.

At the University of Wisconsin–Madison, Dr. David Vail, DVM, is trying to help dogs with oral and digital melanoma (skin cancer). In the current study, he's working on a tumor vaccine that takes the antigens from the tumors, kills off the cancerous tissue, and injects the antigens back into the dog. The antigens then alert the antibodies as to the foreign substance and the body attacks both the antigens and the cancer, destroying the melanoma.

WHAT IS RATIONAL TARGETED THERAPY?

You may hear us use the term *Rational Targeted Therapy* to describe a new form of chemotherapy. Maggie first heard the term from Dr. Philip Bergman (Atwood-Donaldson Cancer Center, Animal Medical Center, New York), who wanted to differentiate the new class of cancer medication from chemotherapy, which has some pretty negative connotations. Unlike the old form of chemotherapy that kills both good cells and bad, the rational targeted therapy is aimed specifically at killing the cancer and sparing the healthy cells. Many of the latest advances use rational targeted therapy rather than the old-style chemotherapy. They generally have fewer side effects and it is hoped they will have better results.

NEW RESEARCH LOOKS AT AVOIDING AMPUTATION WITH OSTEOSARCOMA

Osteosarcoma or bone cancer often requires amputation of the affected leg. Carolyn J. Henry, DVM, of the University of Missouri, is working to possibly change that. Dr. Henry is using both a radioactive chemical called ^{153}Samarium-EDTMP (Quadramet) both as a targeted therapy for patients with bone cancer and as chemotherapy.

Oncologists currently use Quadramet in human patients to relieve cancer pain. The EDTMP allows the Samarium to target bone, thus making this treatment ideal in osteosarcoma. Quadramet's radioactive elements kill the cancer cells, but also bring pain relief in both cancer and arthritis. In some dogs, Quadramet has actually cured early stages of bone cancer.

One of the benefits to combining Quadramet with chemotherapy is that it can work on bone cancer that has metastasized or is in more than one location. Dr. Henry hopes to determine whether they can treat patients with Quadramet and chemotherapy safely and not damage the immune system.

As of this writing, the research is in its second year of a four-year study. Dr. Henry is hoping that this new treatment can provide pain relief and a good quality of life for her patients. The results look promising, so that in the future, dogs may not have to undergo the pain and surgery of bone cancer.

NOT JUST FOR ANIMALS ANYMORE

If you've been paying attention to the latest oncology advances, you may notice that a lot of these studies are leading edge—stuff that you might actually hear about in human medicine as well. And little wonder! Human cancer studies are often teamed with veterinary cancer studies, such as the cancer vaccine research going on with the Donald-Atwood Cancer Center and Sloan-Kettering Medical Center in New York City. In the vaccine tests, both pets and people benefit.

Maggie has her own story to tell about cancer—with her own father. Her father was diagnosed with prostate cancer and underwent surgery and radiation therapy. After a few years, his PSA was elevated, indicating the cancer had returned. He went into a cancer vaccine study, which proved remarkably successful. Two years later, Maggie is happy to report that her dad goes through treatments to knock the cancer back down when his PSA rises. It is a chronic condition but not the life-threatening condition it once was.

The cancer vaccine research made a difference with her dad. Maggie likes to think that veterinary medicine has done its part to save a life—this time, a human one.

NEW RESEARCH IN CHEMOTHERAPY

At UC Davis, veterinary oncologists are working to combat cancer using several innovative anti-cancer medications including SU11654 and a new drug, 2 methoxyestradiol (2-ME2), which is being tested against canine and feline sarcoma, a malignant soft-tissue tumor. Dr. Cheryl A. London, DVM, Ph.D., heads up the UC Davis Cancer Center's Cancer Biology in Animals Program along with Dr. Ron Wisdom, DVM, and is studying both the effects of new drugs on sarcomas and the genetic components that may cause canine malignant histiocytosis in certain breeds such as the Rottweiler, Flat-Coated Retriever, Bernese Mountain Dog, and Golden Retriever.

MRI TO DIAGNOSE LIVER AND SPLEEN TUMORS

At the University of Pennsylvania, Dr. Chick Weisse, VMD, and Dr. Craig Clifford, VMD, are looking for noninvasive ways of diagnosing liver and spleen tumors. Roughly half of the tumors are malignant, but in order to diagnose them, currently they must be biopsied, which requires surgery and anesthesia. Ultrasound may help determine abnormalities in the liver but doesn't necessarily show if the growth is cancerous.

Using MRI, the study has had a 94 percent success rate in determining whether a tumor is malignant or benign. The MRI can also show if the tumor has spread in the abdomen before any surgery. While expensive, this procedure will no doubt aid veterinarians in diagnosing cancer and deciding whether a dog even needs surgery.

HELP FOR HEMANGIOSARCOMA?

At the University of Glasgow, researchers are taking a novel approach to attacking hemangiosarcoma. As you're aware, hemangiosarcoma is a bad cancer with little or no hope for cure. Dr. Lesley Nicholson is looking at identifying peptides (amino acid chains) that bind to hemangiosarcoma cells but leave healthy cells alone. The idea is to introduce a cancer-killing virus that latches onto the hemangiosarcoma and kills it without harming the healthy cells.

At the University of Wisconsin–Madison, Dr. Stuart Helfand is also attacking hemangiosarcoma. Using a form of rational targeted therapy, he's looking at ways to block the growth of cancers cells by inhibiting receptor tyrosine kinases (RTK).

FIGHTING VACCINATION-SITE SARCOMAS IN CATS

One concern cat owners face is the vaccination-site sarcoma. These sarcomas are difficult at best to treat and once a cat has them, the prognosis is not good. Dr. Kenneth Rassnick and his colleagues at Cornell University are investigating using a type of human chemotherapy drug called Ifosfamide that has been proven effective against sarcomas.

The first part of the study showed promise, with two out of twenty-nine cats achieving remission of their fibrosarcomas after just one dose of chemotherapy. The veterinarians are looking into the safety and effectiveness of multiple chemotherapy sessions.

COX-2 INHIBITORS AND SQUAMOUS CELL CARCINOMA

A study completed by Dr. Monique Doré and her colleagues at the University of Montreal studied squamous cell carcinoma and the COX-2 enzyme (the same enzyme that causes arthritis). Through this study, the investigators were able to understand the role of COX-2 in these tumors, which will help researchers develop treatments for inhibiting COX-2 in this cancer.

CISPLATIN / PIROXICAM IN CANINE ORAL CANCER AND BLADDER CANCER

The investigators led by Dr. Deborah W. Knapp, DVM, at Purdue University discovered that combining chemotherapy with NSAIDs achieved a 75 percent remission rate with bladder cancer. Excited by this discovery, the researchers tested dogs with oral cancer and developed a new and relatively safe treatment—even with those dogs who have oral cancers that cannot be operated on.

HOW YOU CAN GET INVOLVED

You can find out more about how to donate to cancer research through the Morris Animal Foundation (www.morrisanimal foundation.org), the AKC Canine Health Foundation (www.akc chf.org), and the Winn-Feline Health Foundation (www.winn felinehealth.org).

SUMMARY

- Veterinary researchers are working to cure cancer or at least make it treatable.
- Various cancer studies have proven to benefit both humans and animals.
- Most studies have given researcher vital peeks into how cancer behaves and what the best course of treatment will be.

CHAPTER

9

Holistic Medicine[1]

IN THIS CHAPTER

- Learn what holistic medicine is.
- Learn if holistic medicine really works.
- Learn what kind of holistic medicine is available to your pets.
- Learn whether you should consider alternative medicine in your pet's treatment.

Case Study

Dusty Rainbolt was surprised by the lump on her cat, Chani's, neck. Chani, a smoke-and-white domestic shorthair, always lay curled up on Dusty when it was bedtime, and Dusty would scratch Chani's chin before drifting off to sleep. This night was different, though. Dusty felt a lump the size of a date on Chani's neck.

"That was back before I did routine health exams," Dusty admitted. "I highly recommend that you examine your pet frequently so you can catch problems."

Worried for her eleven-year-old cat, Dusty took her cat to her vet's where Chani was seen by a substitute vet.

---

1. (From Sources 39, 40, 45, 46, 47, 57, 58, pages 211–215.)

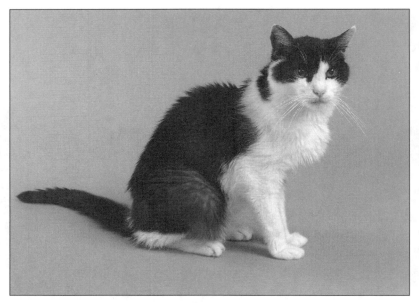

Chani is a miracle kitty who survived hemangiosarcoma.

"*The vet didn't think it was anything, and when she aspirated the lump, all that came out was blood," Dusty said. "She gave me some amoxicillin drops to give to Chani and sent us home. That night, Chani threw up, and I couldn't get the amoxi-drop into her. My husband and I were leaving on a trip the next day, but I knew if I didn't get her treatment, Chani was going to die.*"

Dusty's instincts proved right. She returned to the vet first thing in the morning, and her regular vet decided to remove the lump from Chani's neck and biopsy it while Dusty was out of town. The surgery was difficult, as the tumor was connected to both the carotid artery and the jugular vein. A pathologist diagnosed it as hemangiosarcoma, a rare and exceedingly aggressive cancer in cats.

When Dusty returned home, the vet gave Chani a poor prognosis. The cancer would come back rapidly. Dusty asked her vet if she could try al-

ternative treatments, such as holistic medicine, on her cat. Her vet told her it was all right.

Dusty had a business trip and brought Chani with her to the conference she attended, where there was also a cat show. (Dusty kept Chani in her room where she could closely monitor the cat for any problems.) At one of the booths at the cat show, a woman was selling herbal supplements. Dusty asked the woman for a possible herbal remedy for her cat. The woman handed her two bottles: one of Pau d'arco and the other a Red Clover blend, both manufactured by Nature's Sunshine.

Because the cancer was so aggressive, the vet told Dusty that the cancer would return in a month if not all of it was removed. That night, Dusty started Chani on 1 cc of each herbal blend daily. After she returned home, Dusty had the vet examine Chani for hemangiosarcoma, and the vet found no sign of it. Dusty continued to give Chani the herbal medication for six months with no recurrence of the cancer.

Dusty credits both her vet's skill and the herbal medication for saving Chani's life. In this way, Dusty combined holistic remedies and modern medicine to save the life of her miracle kitty. Chani is now eighteen years old.

WHAT IS HOLISTIC MEDICINE?

Holistic medicine has become very popular in recent years. It goes by several names: alternative medicine, alternative therapies, homeopathic medicine, herbal medicine, holistic medicine, natural medicine, naturopathy, etc. None of these names are correct, nor do they adequately explain what this medicine is. For example, Deb hates the term *holistic medicine* because conventional veterinary medicine also considers the entire animal when making a diagnosis, not just the ailment in question. So, conventional medicine is often holistic in nature.

Some oncologists call certain cancer therapies alternative therapies, but these therapies have nothing to do with what one might term holistic medicine. Homeopathic, herbal, and natural are simply parts of holistic medicine and don't accurately describe it either. (Homeopathy is different from herbal medicine, for example.)

So, what is holistic medicine? (Despite Deb's aversion to using the word, we've decided to use it in this book). According to the American Holistic Veterinary Medical Association, holistic medicine is a ". . . mixture of healing arts and skills . . . as natural as life itself. At the core of this issue lies the very essence of the word '(w)holistic.' It means taking in the whole picture of the patient—the environment, the disease pattern, the relationship of pet with owner—and developing a treatment protocol using a wide range of therapies for healing the patient."

While this is a good definition to start with, it can also fit many practices in conventional (allopathic) medicine. Indeed, many forms of holistic medicine have crept into mainstream veterinary care. Nutraceutical supplements such as glucosamines have made their way into common veterinary practice. Maggie has conventional vets try bottles of herbal remedies along with conventional medicine to help problems like nervousness and to help support kidney and liver functions. Acupuncture and other modalities are recognized through the AVMA as treatments.

What kinds of treatments are available in holistic medicine? These therapies include the following treatments:

- Acupuncture
- Aromatherapy
- Bach Flower Remedies
- Biochemical salts
- Chiropractic

- Cold laser therapy
- Herbal therapies
- Homeopathic
- Light/color therapy
- Magnetic therapy
- Massage
- Nosodes
- Nutrition

Some of these therapies you might recognize as bordering on mainstream. Nutrition, acupuncture, chiropractic, massage, homeopathy, and herbal therapies are all commonplace in our culture. You may have used these therapies on yourself or know of someone who has used them. So, it makes sense to use them on our pets as well.

WEBSITES FOR HOLISTIC MEDICINE

1. American Holistic Veterinary Medication Association— http://www.ahvma.org/
2. American Academy of Veterinary Acupuncture— http://www.aava.org/
3. American Veterinary Chiropractic Association— http://www.animalchiropractic.org/
4. International Association for Veterinary Homeopathy— http://www.iavh.at/
5. International Veterinary Acupuncture Society— http://www.ivas.org/
6. Veterinary Botanical Medical Association— http://www.vbma.org/

HOLISTIC MODALITIES

Acupuncture is a healing art used by the Chinese for over three thousand years. Veterinary acupuncturists can work on a variety of problems such as arthritis, muscle injury, allergy, autoimmune problems, stress, cataracts, and spinal problems.

Aromatherapy uses scents to help healing. Essential oils can be rubbed into the skin and fur or can be dripped into a cup of warm water and placed near the dog's head.

Bach flower remedies are similar to herb therapy and homeopathy, but work with the pet's emotional condition. There are thirty-eight remedies made from flowers, trees, and special waters.

Biochemical salts are electrolytes found in all living things. These minerals are given to patients for a variety of ailments.

Cold Laser/Photon therapy is used primarily for injuries and pain. It stimulates healing.

Veterinary chiropractic deals with diseases caused by spinal interference with normal nerve function. Chiropractic practitioners deal with spinal and bone misalignments that can affect organs, muscles, and gait.

Herbal therapy is used to treat a large number of diseases and to maintain the health of the animal. It can be used both internally and externally depending on the type of herb and condition.

Homeopathy is the use of certain substances that produces a disease's symptoms to cure the disease. Homeopathics dilute the substance, thus enhancing the healing properties and removing the potential poisonous attributes.

Light/color therapy is used for dogs with emotional and biological disorders.

Magnetic therapy is used to help promote healing of fractures and sore muscles and to alleviate arthritis and joint pain.

Massage is intended to alleviate pain and remove toxins.

Nosodes are the homeopathic version of vaccinations.

Nutrition is intended to correct imbalances in diet and help cure and prevent certain diseases.

DOES HOLISTIC MEDICINE WORK?

The answer to whether holistic medicine works is largely debatable, because there is little data that it works, except through anecdotal evidence. Many reputable holistic practitioners agree that some things termed "holistic medicine" are downright quackery and that there are many unscrupulous people in the field. But there are many veterinarians who do know holistic medicine and who are certified in certain modalities. There are also many holistic therapies that seem to work even though we don't understand exactly why.

Until there are double-blind studies that are peer reviewed, we probably won't know conclusively whether certain forms of holistic medicine work. However, there seems to be enough anecdotal evidence to suggest some things do indeed work. Maggie has used holistic medicines on her pets with positive results, but has never used these holistic therapies for cancer.

Indeed, both authors recommend that in a situation such as cancer, you should first seek the advice of a veterinary oncologist. In many cases, cancer can be cured through conventional methods, provided the cancer is caught early and the conventional method applied. While holistic medicine may affect cancer, an all too common scenario is that the pet's owner opts for holistic medicine rather than conventional medicine, only to have the cancer progress to a point where not even conventional medicine will work.

While most holistic medicine can be used in conjunction with conventional cancer treatments, occasionally holistic therapies may interfere. This is another reason to talk with the oncologist before applying any holistic modalities—to make sure that by giving holistic treatment you're not undoing the work the oncologist is doing.

When deciding to take your dog or cat to a holistic practitioner, be certain that the person you're using is a licensed veterinarian. While there are many good people practicing holistic medicine without a veterinary degree, there are many who are not trustworthy and who are taking advantage of people at a vulnerable time. The benefit to choosing a vet who is also experienced in different holistic modalities is that the vet can switch from allopathic (conventional) medicine to holistic medicine and back again as required. He should be willing to work with a veterinary oncologist if the cancer is more serious than a growth or a tumor.

Usually a holistic veterinarian uses a combination of modalities. We'll take a look at the various treatments for cancer.

HOMEOPATHY

Homeopathy uses a miniscule amount of a substance that produces a disease's symptoms to cure the disease. Dr. Samuel Hahnemann, M.D., developed homeopathy in 1790. He discovered that certain substances that produced a disease's symptoms could cure the disease. By diluting the substance, the healing properties are greatly enhanced and the potential poisonous attributes are removed.

The concept of "like curing like" may seem a little odd. The idea that something that causes you to have a fever could cure a fever doesn't make much sense to today's logic, but that's exactly what homeopathy works with. What's more, the smaller the amount used, the more potent the medication is. So a homeopathic medication that has been diluted thirty times is more powerful than one diluted only ten times.

When a homeopathic medicine is made, one part of the substance is put in with nine parts of whatever is diluting it (usually distilled water). The mixture is then succussed (that is, shaken by turning over and over vigorously) to release the energies of the substance. A mixture that is produced in this way is considered 1X strength.

When you take a mixture that is 1X and dilute it with nine parts of the diluting substance and succuss it, it is now 2X. Dilute the 2X mixture with nine parts and succuss it and it is now 3X, and so on. Some homeopathic remedies are mixed over a hundred times and show 1C, 2C, etc. (C means 100 times.) Those C homeopathic medicines are more powerful than the X medications, even though they are more dilute.

One of the benefits to homeopathic medicine is that it's extremely safe. Because the dangerous qualities of the original substance are diluted, there's no chance of getting ill from them. (For example, substances such as arsenic and belladonna [deadly nightshade] are downright lethal even in smaller doses, but the dilution and succussing removes all toxicity.)

A variety of homeopathic medications is available, and you should consider talking with a trained veterinary homoeopathist to determine what the best medication is for your pet.

HERBAL THERAPY

Humans have used healing herbs since long before recorded history. Throughout the ages, teas and poultices have been used to heal. Only recently have people rediscovered herbs and their healing properties. This is strange when you consider that many of today's medications have their "roots" in herbs and plants.

One of the downsides to using herbs is the lack of oversight in companies that produce herbal supplements. At the time of this writing, the FDA does not oversee what are considered "nutritional supplements." This is especially true in herbs where the company may or may not adhere to any particular standard.

Another problem with herbs is determining a precise dosage. Potency varies from plant to plant, and without some type of standard, you can't really know how much you may be giving your pet. Too much and you may be overdosing, too little and it's ineffectual.

Last, the herb itself may interfere with your pet's allopathic treatment. Your vet may or may not know how a particular herb is converted in your pet's body or whether that herb will interfere with medication. For example, St. John's Wort, commonly used as an antidepressant, can actually reduce the effectiveness of many medications and should never be used with antidepressants known as MAOIs.

When looking at the following list of herbs, please realize that the herbs are purported to have these effects and that neither the authors nor the publisher can vouch for the healing qualities nor the safety of these herbs.

- *Aloe Vera* is said to help fight infections and cancer.
- *Cat's Claw (una de gato)* is a Brazilian herb that is purported to shrink tumors.
- *Chaparral* is a desert plant said to treat tumors.
- *Chinese Astragalus* is an herb said to boost the immune system, thus making the animal's body fight off the cancer.
- *Essiac tea* is a mixture of herbs including burdock, Indian rhubarb, sorrel, and slippery elm.
- *Hoxsey* is a mixture of poke root, barberry root, burdock root, stillinga root, and buckthorn bark. When mixed as a salve with bloodroot, it is applied to the area above the tumor.
- *Milk thistle* is said to help liver function.
- *Pau d'arco* is a Brazilian herb that is said to boost the immune system and that has cancer-fighting properties.

➤ *Red clover* is said to have cancer-fighting properties.

➤ *Saw palmetto* is said to work for prostate cancer in dogs.

➤ *Tumeric* is an herb said to have strong anti-inflammatory properties that also boosts the immune system.

➤ *Tian xian* is a Chinese herbal supplement to fight cancer.

If you're planning on using herbal medications, it's best to talk with a veterinarian skilled in herbal therapy so he or she can recommend the correct course of treatment for your pet's cancer.

NUTRITION MODALITY

In recent studies done by veterinarians such as Dr. Greg Ogivilie, DVM, tumors and cancer have been shown to thrive on simple carbohydrates and blood sugars. Animals who were fed diets that avoided simple carbohydrates effectively "starved" the tumors. Furthermore, some polyunsaturated fats, most notably Omega-3's and docohexaenoic acid (DHA) inhibit the tumor's growth and may actually improve the results of chemotherapy and radiation therapy.

What does this mean for pet the owner who has a cancer patient? By reducing carbohydrates while increasing proteins and polyunsaturated fats, you may be able to help shrink tumors or help inhibit the cancer. Hill's Science Diet Canine n/d® was formulated as a cancer diet due to this research.

One interesting note in the fight against cancer is the use of antioxidants such as Vitamin C, Vitamin E, Coenzyme Q10, Beta carotene, pycnogenol, IP-6 (Vitamin B insitol), and Alpga-lipoic acid. Before dosing your pet with these, consider that certain treatments such as chemotherapy actually produce free radicals, which antioxidants destroy. At the wrong dosages, these antioxidants can be dangerous to your pet, so consult with a veterinarian before using these.

ACUPUNCTURE

Acupuncture is probably the most accepted form of alternative medicine. And little wonder! It had been practiced for thousands of years in China before making its way to the United States. According to Eastern medicine, the body has a *Chi* or *Qi*, a central life force. This Chi radiates across the body in the form of meridians. When something blocks the flow of the Chi, it causes pain and disease. Using needles, acupuncture works to unblock the flow of the Chi and maintain balance.

That's the theory according to Eastern medicine. Whether you choose to believe it is the Chi or that acupuncture somehow works with nerves or through stimulating biochemicals in the body, most people agree it does work in some fashion, so much so that the American Veterinary Medical Association recognizes it as well.

Acupuncture can help your pet with pain and can also aid in recovery times (from surgery, radiation, or chemotherapy). Maggie has seen pets (and has had her own dog) undergo acupuncture with positive results. The needles cause less sensation than a mosquito bite when they're first inserted. Indeed, most dogs and cats seem to enjoy the treatment and many will stand still or lie down while looking like a pincushion.

There are some risks associated with acupuncture, which is why it's important to have a veterinarian certified in acupuncture. Needles must be for one-time use only and should be sterile to prevent the spread of disease (in most practices, this is the case). Infections and broken needles are rare, but can occur. In extreme cases with long needles, there's a chance of hitting an organ.

Contact the American Academy of Veterinary Acupuncture (AAVA) or the International Veterinary Acupuncture Society (IVAS) for a listing of veterinarians in your area who are certified veterinary acupuncturists. The AVMA may also be a resource in looking for veterinarians who practice acupuncture as well as conventional medicine.

SHOULD YOU CONSIDER ALTERNATIVE MEDICINE?

Should you use holistic or alternative medicine to treat your pet? When dealing with cancer, a person's first inclination is to throw everything they can at the problem and hope it cures it. After all, you want your pet to be well!

But not all holistic medicine is good, depending on the disease and the prescribed course of treatment. As we said before, choosing to use holistic medicine instead of conventional medicine may prove disastrous. You should always talk with your vet before trying holistic treatments on your pet to be sure that the treatments will not interfere with what the vet or veterinary oncologist is trying to accomplish.

When looking into holistic medicine, remember that natural isn't always better. There are plenty of natural poisons in the wild, and not everything is beneficial. Also, be aware that many medicines we use now are synthesized versions of the natural forms. In their natural form, certain medicines may vary widely. You can overdose or underdose a pet, or you might be giving an herb that the body transforms into other medications. For example, yucca is transformed into a substance similar to prednisolone in the body. Prednisolone is a steroid that reduces inflammation but also suppresses the immune system. You can possibly interfere with a cancer vaccine treatment (which intends to stimulate the immune system) by giving yucca. This is one more reason to list with your vet all the herbals and supplements your pet is on!

We feel that holistic medicine works best in situations where a vet or oncologist believes that there's no harm in using it and it can help make the difference between a successful treatment and recovery and one that is either painful for the animal or where the cancer returns. These situations may include (but are not limited to) pain management, limited conventional treatment options, follow-up care, and increasing a pet's stamina to handle treatments and recovery. Because there is no scientific proof that certain modalities work, substituting holistic medicine for conventional medicine may in fact be very dangerous to your pet. Certain cancers that can be cured or put into remission by conventional means may not react to certain holistic treatments. Recognition of the pet owner's error may come too late for conventional medicine to do anything about it.

SUMMARY

- Many alternative therapies are available for someone who wishes to do more for a sick pet.
- Be cautious when looking for practitioners of holistic medicines—be certain that the practitioner is a veterinarian.
- Talk with your veterinarian and veterinary oncologist before using holistic medicine. Some holistic medicine is contraindicated when treating your pet with certain types of conventional therapies.
- Do not substitute holistic medicine for conventional cancer treatments, especially if there is a high success rate with the conventional methods.
- Holistic medicine is best used as complementary medicine for your pet.

10

Decision Making

IN THIS CHAPTER
- Learn how to make informed decisions when it comes to the care of your pet.
- Learn what monetary options are available to you to finance your pet's cancer care.
- Learn how to find out what options are available for your pet's treatment.

Receiving a diagnosis of cancer can be a traumatic experience for the pet owner. Now that it is confirmed that your pet has cancer, it's time to make some tough decisions. Friends, family members, veterinarians, and even complete strangers on the Internet may have advice for you. Not all of the advice is sound, and some shouldn't factor at all into the decision you make for your pet.

You need to gather information from *reliable* sources. This includes information obtained from your veterinarian, diagnostic tests, specialists, and from reliable sources on the Internet, such as verifiable veterinary websites. You will also have to determine whether the treatment will improve the quality of life of your pet as well as lengthen his life. Can your pet eat, eliminate, and breathe comfortably? Will he tolerate treatment? Does the discomfort now potentially mean long years of health? Can you afford the treatment? What treatment is best?

In this chapter, we look at critical decision making—how to talk to your veterinarian regarding care of your pet; how to look for the information necessary to make the right decision; what options are available to pay for treatment if you don't have the financial means. Hopefully, these suggestions will help you make decisions in treating your pet with cancer.

CRITICAL DECISION MAKING

When you have a pet with cancer, you are faced with some very serious and tough decisions. You need to prepare yourself with information so you can make the right decisions. You need medical information, personal information, and financial information.

The diagnosis of cancer should be confirmed by a biopsy or a positive finding on a fine needle aspirate. Don't accept a plain x-ray without further information. You need to know what kind of cancer you are dealing with and the stage or level of malignancy, if possible.

Check the Internet, but also realize that anyone can post anything on the Internet. Look for websites of board certified veterinarians, the Veterinary Cancer Society, and veterinary colleges. The American Veterinary Medical Association and the American Animal Hospital Association both have excellent sites for consumers.

Once you have as much diagnostic information as possible, look at the overall health of your pet. Along with a thorough physical examination, expect your vet to do a urinalysis, complete blood count (CBC), and a complete blood panel to evaluate your pet's liver, kidneys, and general health. A dog with kidney failure will have a much more difficult time handling chemotherapy and treatments than a dog with healthy kidneys. A chest x-ray will screen for any obvious metastases (spread of the cancer) to the lungs. You need to know this information ahead of time to adjust treatment options.

The health information you have gathered is easy to evaluate compared with the subjective factors. You need to look at your pet to determine objectively how much pain she might be in. Look at the quality of life she has right now; think about the stresses of cancer therapies, and go beyond that to the hoped-for results. If your dog is fifteen years old and treatment will take six months and give him perhaps an extra four months beyond that, you may decide it is not justified. He may not live beyond a few more months even without the cancer. Evaluate any gains in quantity of time versus the quality of life. What good are six extra months if your pet has to be hospitalized for four of those months? On the other hand, if your pet is young and six months of treatment could give her years more of quality life, that is a very different scenario.

If therapy involves a leg amputation, you need to know if the other joints in your pet's body are healthy enough to handle the extra work. Additional x-rays may be required to evaluate those joints. How painful will treatment be and what are the odds for a pain-free existence post-therapy?

There may be a wide range of treatment options for the cancer your pet has. Look at what treatments are feasible for your pet and for you. If there is a new surgery being attempted, but it is done only at a site across the country, can you realistically travel that far? Could your pet handle separation? How does your pet handle getting injections or being given pills? How much nursing care can you provide? Are there limits on your time or abilities? If your pet won't handle the treatments, the decisions may be out of your hands.

And sadly, economics is often a factor in our equations. Can you afford to have this cancer treated in the best possible way? With diseases such as cancer, the best treatment options are often to do "everything" or to do nothing but hospice care. Sometimes treatment plans in between those extremes are reasonable options, but not always.

The factors you need to consider in your critical decision making are:

- Exact diagnosis (or at least as exact as you can come up with)
- Overall health of your pet
- Prognosis in terms of both quantity of time and quality of life
- Treatment options
- Economics

TALKING ABOUT OPTIONS WITH YOUR VETERINARIAN—MAKING AN INFORMED DECISION

Once you have your information, sit down with your veterinarian and develop a plan for your individual pet. Don't let the decisions of other pet owners influence you—you know your pet better than anyone else. Often, the degrees of cancer are different even in pets with the same diagnosis.

You should have a list of questions for your veterinarian after you have a definitive diagnosis. You need to know about the treatment options—ranging from the best and most complete to the comfort care and hospice options. Don't be shy! Ask hard questions about how treatment will affect your pet, what side effects you can expect, what are the odds of success. Bring along any information you have researched yourself. You have more time to search the Internet for your one pet than your veterinarian who is caring for many pets. Remember, though—always read information on the Internet with a critical eye. Not all information on the Internet is factual or correct.

Realize as you ask these questions that medicine is not an exact science. There may not be black and white answers to some of your questions. Your veterinarian may give you a wide range of answers and some of those may be her best "guesstimates." While your regular veterinarian may have an interest in treating cancers, you should consult with a board certified veterinarian or even a team of board certified veterinarians. Most board certified surgeons and internists have extensive experience with cancer treatments. Almost all pets with cancer come under the treatment of a veterinary specialist, even if just by phone consultations. You may request more than one referral opinion if you are not comfortable with the first specialist. Your veterinarian can arrange these referrals and consultations for you. You will be putting a great deal of time, money and emotional input into the care and treatment of your pet. Make sure you are dealing with veterinarians you are comfortable with and who share your philosophy about the care of your pet.

You will probably be speaking with a specialist as well as your personal veterinarian. Some specialists prefer to deal with your veterinarian and you as a team. Others may want to just communicate with just one of you. Make sure you are clear about your access to your pet's veterinarian so you know whom to contact if you have problems.

Your veterinarian will try to guide you in your decision making—perhaps bringing up examples of other pets who have had similar diseases. He cannot make the decisions for you, however.

Be very open and frank with your veterinarian and the specialist about finances. You can easily be looking at expenses in the thousands of dollars. Most clinics will try to arrange payment options, but you need to set that up ahead of time. See the section on the cost of veterinary care and treatment later in this chapter.

QUESTIONS FOR YOUR VETERINARIAN

The following are questions you should ask your veterinarian when making an informed decision on treatment:

- What treatment options are available from the complete attack on this cancer to hospice options?
- What are the likely side effects that my pet will experience from the various treatments?
- If I elect only hospice care, what am I likely to see in terms of life quality and life expectancy?
- What sort of prognosis will my pet have with treatment? These odds will vary greatly with the treatment options, the overall health of your pet to begin with, and the exact type of cancer your pet has.
- What are the financial costs of the various options?

SEEKING COUNSELING

Seeking counseling when your pet has cancer may sound extravagant, but it's good advice for anyone who must face tough decisions such as whether to treat a pet aggressively or opt for euthanasia. Quite often, the owner is flooded with a variety of opinions as to what he or she should do. Everyone from the veterinarian to family members to people on the Internet have an opinion as to what course of action is best for the pet. An unbiased counselor can provide guidance in choosing the best course of action for the person and situation.

Counseling doesn't have to be expensive either. Many veterinary colleges and some hospitals, such as the Animal Medical Center in New York, have counselors available. While most are there for bereavement counseling, a few will provide counseling free for pet owners faced with difficult decisions.

Talk with your veterinarian. He or she may be able to suggest counseling groups in your area or provide hotline numbers. At the Animal Medical Center, all Human-Animal Bond Programs are offered free of charge. Counselors are available for individual sessions, phone consultation, and support groups. For more information, contact The Animal Medical Center, Human-Animal Bond Programs, 510 East 62nd Street, New York NY 10021-8383, (212) 838-8100. You can also find support hotline numbers at www.petloss.com.

THE COST OF VETERINARY CARE

If you've owned a pet for any length of time, you've had to visit the veterinarian and pay for procedures. You can expect a larger bill for cancer treatment. After all, a simple check-up and vaccinations may cost fifty dollars or more; cancer treatment is more specialized. Have a series of tests run or an operation, and you're likely to see a bill in the hundreds of dollars. Some operations and care go into the thousands of dollars.

Veterinary care is cheaper than the equivalent human health care, and yet it requires the same expertise. In cancer treatment, veterinarians are performing the same operations and treatments at a fraction of the cost that humans would pay. If you compare the cost of the last time you went to see the doctor (what your insurance paid, if you have it) with what your veterinarian charges, you'll see that veterinary care is relatively affordable

When paying for an oncologist, you are paying for that veterinarian's expertise. The veterinarian is a professional and his schooling is just as intensive as a human oncologist's. Your vet has a practice to pay for, including the business space, the equipment, and the cost of supplies. He or she may have a family to support.

Even so, this isn't much comfort when you discover that to treat the cancer in your beloved pet aggressively may cost well over a thousand dollars. Caught between euthanizing a pet or facing a bill they can't possibly afford, many pet owners have sadly opted for euthanasia.

Having to make that dreadful choice is something no pet owner wants to face. However, there are options for the pet owner, including low-cost research alternatives, pet health insurance, and payment plans and options.

Determining How Much You Can Afford

Before you begin any treatment on your pet, you should consider how much you can reasonably afford to pay. We often think of our beloved pets as family members (many are), and we'll do whatever it takes to treat them. However, this may not be realistic if you don't have much disposable income.

Come up with a number you can realistically pay up front and over time. The up-front cost is important because surgery and certain procedures can become expensive in a relatively short time. The over time figure can be used for treatments over several months. This will help you be ready to discuss options with your veterinarian or veterinary oncologist when he or she talks to you about treatment options.

Talking to Your Veterinarian about Expenses

Most people feel uncomfortable talking about finances with their veterinarian. No one wants to sound cheap when it comes to their pet's care, but if you can't afford to pay for diagnostics or specialized treatments, it's better to say so up front. Diagnostic tests, surgery, chemotherapy, radiation, and other procedures can be pricey, and many owners are ill informed on how much these procedures cost.

Once the veterinarian knows your financial situation, he or she may suggest alternate courses of action in diagnosing and treating the cancer or tumor. Others may offer payment plans or financing. Others may be able to recommend lower-cost clinics that can offer you discounts.

Veterinary Medical Insurance

Pet health insurance or veterinary medical insurance is equivalent to human health insurance. Pet health insurance began in 1980 with the debut of VPI or Veterinary Pet Insurance. Since then, a number of pet health insurance plans have appeared—some offering HMO or PPO-type services, others offering major medical, and still others offering a discount rate.

There are two major problems with pet health insurance. The first is that most do not cover preexisting conditions. If you're reading this book, chances are your pet already has cancer, and buying coverage now will not help you. Second, pet health insurance companies come and go, so if you decide to purchase a plan, be certain to choose an insurance that is underwritten by a company that is rated A or higher. Longevity is also important. The worst thing that could happen is that you pay for insurance and the company goes under before you can get a claim paid.

If you do purchase a plan, be certain to read and understand the exclusions and caps. Some insurances cap how much they're willing to pay out per illness, and some won't pay for "experimental procedures." Still others may have exclusions for types of illnesses—including cancer. Insurance premiums increase as your pet becomes older. There may be age limitations as well.

PET HEALTH INSURANCE

The following is a list of pet health insurance plans. The authors in no way endorse these plans and have included them for informational purposes only:

Pet Assure
10 South Morris St
Dover, NJ 07801
888-789-PETS (7387)
Email: custserv@petassure.com
Website: http://www.petassure.com/

PetCare Insurance Programs
PO Box 8575
Rolling Meadows, IL 60008-8575
E-mail: info@petcareinsurance.com
Website: http://www.petcareinsurance.com/us/

Pet Plan Insurance (Canada)
777 Portage Ave
Winnipeg, MB R3G 0N3 CANADA
905-279-7190
Website: http://www.petplan.com/

Petshealth Insurance Agency
PO Box 2847
Canton, OH 44720
888-592-7387
Website: http://www.petshealthplan.com/

Premier Pet Insurance Group
9541 Harding Blvd
Wauwatosa, WI 53226

877-774-2273
Website: http://www.ppins.com/

Veterinary Pet Insurance (VPI)
P.O. Box 2344
Brea, CA 92822-2344
800-USA-PETS
Website: http://www.petinsurance.com/

Alternatives to Veterinary Medical Insurance

Alternatives to pet health insurance include savings plans and financing. Some veterinarians offer savings plans where you can put away money to use later. Others will allow you to pay off the medical costs over time. Still others may be able to offer a loan or financing plan through various financial institutions.

If you're unable to obtain financing or don't have a savings plan, you can look for financial assistance from local animal organizations. Sometimes funds are available to handle emergencies or involved treatments. Ask your veterinarian or local animal shelters for possible referrals.

Low-Cost Research Alternatives

Sometimes you can obtain low-cost or even free medical care through studies at veterinary colleges. To enable you to participate, your veterinarian will have to contact the American Veterinary Cancer Society or colleges that participate in cancer research studies to find out if your pet qualifies for research.

In some studies, the animal must visit the research facility occasionally for testing and treatment. In other studies, your veterinarian may be able to treat your pet and submit biopsy and other test results to the research facility. In either case, your pet may receive the necessary treatment.

The downside to this research is that the treatment may not help your pet at all. Or your pet may be in the control group—that is, he may not receive the experimental treatment. Talk with your veterinarian and the researchers about what treatment your pet may receive. However, the benefits to research may far outweigh the negatives and your pet may have access to some of the most leading edge treatment available.

SUMMARY

Making decisions about critical care for a pet with cancer can be emotionally draining and difficult. Listing the information you need to help you in decision making can be helpful.

- Medical information
  - Diagnosis
  - Overall health of your pet
  - Prognosis (most likely outcome)
  - Treatment options
- Professional help
  - Your veterinarian
  - Specialists in pet cancer care and treatment
  - Counselors
- Finances
  - Available funds
  - Pet health insurance
  - Other sources

11

Euthanasia

IN THIS CHAPTER
- Learn when to make the decision to euthanize your pet.
- Learn what the stages of grief are.
- Learn ways to memorialize your pet.
- Learn how to get help during your grieving period.

Euthanasia is a tough subject for most pet owners to deal with. Most of us don't like thinking about death, and the death of our beloved animals is often too much for us to contemplate. But the sad fact is that most of us will outlive our pets. Cancer is a wake-up call to our dogs' and cats' mortality.

The hard part is when to let go. When should you make the decision to euthanize your dog or cat? And when you do decide to euthanize, is it all right to grieve? Last, in this chapter we cover memorials to your pet and also whether you should get another pet to help with the loss.

Case Study

On January 7, 1999, Lin Battaglia found lumps under Pepper's chin. Pepper was a beautiful sable and white Sheltie who had been Lin's birthday

Pepper's death inspired a memorial fund.

present almost seven years before. The veterinarian's prognosis was grim: Pepper had Stage III canine lymphoma.

"I take care of my dogs," Lin says. "I check them regularly and do blood panels on them every year before putting them through something strenuous like agility." Lin, a dog trainer and behaviorist and owner of mdt-Agility Ability, has several dogs, but none was as special as Pepper. "Pepper was named that because my son saw him and said 'He's just like a little chili pepper.' He was a rowdy and excited puppy."

Pepper lived up to his name, earning multiple titles in agility, obedience, and herding. He became the first therapy dog in Reno, Nevada, and touched many people's lives with his gentleness and understanding. "He had an innate quality of knowing what to do to win people over. If the kids required a rowdy and playful dog, he'd be that way. If the person was scared of dogs, he would be slow and gentle."

Lin did everything she could to save Pepper's life. She drove Pepper once a week from Reno to Sacramento, California—three hours or more in the winter—to make his chemotherapy appointments, spending over $13,000. "He deserved a chance."

Pepper competed in agility and continued to earn titles until a month before he died. Lin would do blood work before the trial to determine if he could handle the strain. "Agility was very important to his psyche. To take agility away from him would've been too cruel."

Ten months after being diagnosed, Pepper passed away at home with his family on November 15, 1999. In 2001, Lin and Greg Battaglia established the Pepper Memorial Cancer Fund with the Morris Animal Foundation. That April, Lin ran the first Pepper Memorial Classic Agility Trial. This first agility trial earned $6,000 in proceeds that were donated to the Morris Animal Foundation.

As of this writing, Pepper Memorial Classic Agility Trial is in its fourth year. In the second and third year, it earned $8,000 each year. They have a raffle and silent auction that add to the donations and entries. "This agility trial is different than any other agility trial," says Lin. "The trial fills up in a day and a half and is limited to one hundred dogs. It brings everyone together who has been touched by cancer. We call out the names of the dogs we've lost at the trial. It's very emotional."

Lin believes that Pepper lives on in the trial. "Pepper is here and running with every dog. We've had dogs who couldn't qualify the entire year qualify at this trial."

For Lin, the money earned is small. "Cancer studies cost over $40,000. It's our small way. Just think if everyone in NADAC were to contribute just one dollar to cancer research. We would have $100,000."

For Lin, this is a small part of keeping Pepper's memory alive. "I wanted to make losing Pepper stand for something," says Lin. "There's always one dog that touches you—a soul-mate. Pepper was mine."

SHOULD YOU EUTHANIZE?

Euthanasia is possibly the toughest decision you'll ever have to make concerning your pet. Most of us are very attached to our pets—many of us have experienced "heart dogs" or "heart cats" in our lives—those animals who are more important to us than many people we know. The thought of losing someone we consider our closest friend or our furry kid is almost too hard to bear. But the fact remains that the lives of dogs and cats are shorter than ours—and cancer may make them shorter still. When is the right time to put an end to suffering?

Veterinarians and veterinary hospitals are becoming more in tune with pet owners' needs for counseling to make the right decision. In some places like the Animal Medical Center in New York City, veterinary hospitals have counselors available at no charge to discuss your pet's health and help you arrive at the best decision for your situation.

When deciding whether or not to euthanize, you may want to take the following factors into consideration:

- Is your pet suffering?
- Will the treatment prove beneficial to your pet and improve the quality of his life?
- Will the treatment gains outweigh the potential pain associated with the treatment?
- Does the treatment have a good prognosis?
- Can your pet enjoy life?
- Is he able to breathe, eat, urinate, defecate, and move around easily?

- Can you afford the treatment?
- Are you keeping your pet alive for his sake or yours?

In most cases, if the pet is in pain and there is very little the treatment can do beyond prolonging the misery, you should consider euthanasia. Talk with your vet honestly about the prognosis and treatment options—as well as pain management. Palliative treatment *is* an acceptable option as long as you can keep your pet pain-free and comfortable, so don't overlook it. At the same time, don't think you can always buy time with palliative care—Maggie's beloved Alaskan Malamute, Kiana, had to be put down after four days of palliative treatment because the cancer had become so painful it overwhelmed the medication.

If your veterinarian doesn't want to commit to a recommendation, you may have to seek help elsewhere in making your decision. In this case, Maggie's veterinarian recommended when euthanasia was advisable, but also provided other options. Deb notes that many of her clients who finally choose euthanasia remark that they've waited too long, whereas she hasn't known anyone who has said that they euthanized too soon. Loving owners tend to hang onto their pets as long as possible.

One of the most heart-wrenching decisions a pet owner can face is whether to euthanize because the cancer treatments are far beyond anything you can afford. Let's be honest here—if you're looking at cancer that has metastasized, you're likely to be looking at some pretty hefty veterinary bills. However, there are low-cost or relatively free studies that may provide hope if you find you can't pay for treatments (see chapter 10).

Whatever your decision, don't allow your best friend to suffer needlessly. Too often, we're caught up with the potential promise of a breakthrough in veterinary care and aren't realistic about a poor prognosis. While it is tempting to try heroic actions to save your pet, you may discover that the result is still the same. Cats and dogs don't live forever, and even though you want your pet to live a little longer, it may not be humane or in anyone's capacity.

One thing to be aware of is that your pet doesn't understand why he's going through pain. Unlike humans, who can understand that the pain we go through in treatments is for our own good, dogs and cats have no concept of this. Your pet may trust you, but he can't understand that the pain he suffers now may help him.

Euthanasia is painless and quick. The veterinarian will administer an injection and your pet will be gone. You can stay with your pet during his final minutes or leave—it's your choice. Many pet owners opt to stay with their pet during the last few minutes because it brings closure.

SEEKING COUNSELING

During this trying time, you're going to hear a lot of opinions. Your vet may tell you to do one thing; your oncologist may tell you something else. Your family and friends will add their opinions. Acquaintances and coworkers may make more suggestions. If you're on the Internet, you may get recommendations from strangers. And if you've been reading this book, no doubt our recommendations have influenced you as well. What do you do?

Before you follow any recommendations, be sure to get the facts. If you trust your vet and the oncologist who are working on your pet as the experts, be sure to ask them what the prognosis is and whether or not a particular treatment is effective. Ask for their honest assessments of your pet's health and her chances of maintaining a good quality of life. Discuss palliative care and euthanasia as an option. Given the circumstances, does it make sense?

If your vet is unwilling or unable to make that assessment, the next step is to seek counseling. Some pet loss grief counselors are also trained to help in critical decision making and are available at no or low cost. Sometimes talking with an impartial person who has nothing to gain or lose in the situation can help you see things clearly. It's okay to talk to a counselor—they often offer an unbiased opinion that may make the most sense. See *Available Counseling* in the next section.

THE GRIEVING PROCESS

Grief is something we as humans must deal with when faced with our beloved pet's death. Grieving for a pet is much like grieving for a beloved family member—you will feel sadness just as though you're grieving for the loss of a human loved one. There's no shame in this—both Maggie and Deb have grieved for pets they've lost over the years.

Grief is a very complex emotion, so complex that psychologists have identified stages of grief that we all go through. Although they're given various names and phases, they generally fit five or six categories. These include shock, anger, denial, guilt, depression, and acceptance. Let's look at the six stages:

- **Shock**—You can't believe this is happening and don't know what to do. This is a natural reaction to something unpleasant.
- **Anger**—You may be angry at yourself, your veterinarian, or your pet. You may be angry at God or the universe for doing this to your pet. You may blame your veterinarian or the oncologist for not saving your pet. Nevertheless, your temper can become hair-trigger.
- **Denial**—You may decide to deal with your pet's death by simply refusing to believe she's gone. You hold out hope that she'll come bounding through the door into your arms or that she's actually beside you, but you just don't see her.

- **Guilt**—You think that maybe if you had done something different it would change the outcome. "If only I had . . ." you may say, when in reality there may or may not have been anything anyone could have done.
- **Depression**—You may experience depression, crying often, having trouble sleeping and eating, withdrawing from other people and activities, and maybe even having thoughts of suicide. You may try to bargain with the universe or God to get your beloved pet back.
- **Acceptance**—You accept that your pet has died. The sadness persists, but you are willing to let go. You're now remembering the good and the bad times with your pet and you are willing to move on.

As you read through the stages, you might recognize yourself in these descriptions. Many people go through the stages in this order, but may vacillate between the stages or may skip stages. For example, when you hear your dog has cancer, you may go through shock ("Oh, my God!") and denial ("He can't be sick—look at him playing!"). This may be followed by guilt ("Why didn't I see something was wrong?") or anger ("This is all the vet's fault!"). Indeed, a person may fluctuate between these emotions and reactions.

There is no set time period for how long a person goes through grieving. It's not as if you can set a timer and say "Now, I'm going from guilt to depression and next month I'll be in acceptance." It just doesn't work that way.

When going through the stages of grief, it's good to seek counseling. It's not a sign that you're weak or unable to "deal with" your pet's death. Often the counselor can help you see things you might not have seen because you've been full of guilt and anger. Talking to someone is very therapeutic, too. It's not good to keep grief penned up inside you, because it can affect your other relationships, your work, and even your health.

Take care of yourself during this time. Eat the right foods, exercise, and try to get enough sleep. Remember to do things that are fun for you during normal times. Eventually, you will get through this trying time. A new dog or cat may be able to distract you—as will a new project or work. But be careful about bringing a new pet into your house too soon. Sometimes people are quick to compare the new pet with the old one. (See *Another Dog or Cat?* later in this chapter.)

AVAILABLE COUNSELING

Grief is natural when faced with the death of one's pet. Some pet owners are closer to their pets than to many people. Pet loss support counselors understand that in many circumstances, friends, coworkers, and even family members may not be the best people to talk to. Often these people don't understand the special relationship between pets and their owners. They try to cheer up the grieving person—or worse, tell the person that his or her beloved pet was "just a dog" or "just a cat."

Pet loss support groups can help pet owners overcome the overwhelming grief associated with the loss of a pet. Talking with others in the same situation helps owners recognize that they are not alone in their grief and that their feelings are normal. Counseling is available for free or for the cost of a phone call at many veterinary universities and larger veterinary hospitals.

All Human-Animal Bond Programs at The Animal Medical Center in New York are offered free of charge and run through donations. Counselors are available for individual sessions, phone consultation, and support groups. For more info, contact The Animal Medical Center, Human-Animal Bond Programs, 510 East 62nd Street, New York NY 10021-8383, (212) 838-8100.

Ask your vet for possible pet loss support groups or resources. If your vet doesn't have any recommendations, you can contact local veterinary colleges, humane societies, or even universities or colleges with counselors who are pet lovers.

If you experience suicidal or other potentially destructive feelings, seek professional help immediately. A trained therapist can help you get beyond these feelings and perhaps find an underlying medical condition.

GRIEF AND CHILDREN

If your dog or cat is a beloved family pet, your whole family may go into bereavement. This often includes children, who may not understand the concept of death and their pet.

When talking to a child, it's best to be honest concerning the death of a pet. Don't tell her that God wanted Fluffy in heaven, because that will just scare the child into thinking that God will take her too. Don't lie either—don't tell her that her pet has run away or that you've given her to a good home. At some point, your child will have to understand that the beloved pet is gone and won't be coming back. (If you believe that dogs and cats go to heaven, it is perfectly ok to tell the child that).

Encourage your child to express her feelings about the pet's death. Sometimes drawing a picture or building some type of memorial will help the child work through the feelings of grief.

Maggie remembers seeing a school bus run over a friend's cat as a child. It was very traumatic. Both she and her friend buried the cat in the backyard, and her friend talked to her about her cat. By listening, Maggie learned about pet loss and how to be a good friend.

INTERNET LINKS TO COUNSELING AND PET LOSS SITES

- The Animal Medical Center, Human-Animal Bond discussion group http://www.amcny.org
- Rainbow Bridge http://www.alaska.net/~bearpaw/rainbow.htm
- Association for Pet Loss and Bereavement http://www.aplb.org
- The Pet Loss Grief Support Website http://www.petloss.com
- The Virtual Pet Cemetery http://www.lavamind.com/pet.html
- Cornell University Pet Loss Support Website—http://web.vet.cornell.edu/public/petloss/

PET LOSS SUPPORT PHONE HOTLINES

- Cornell Pet Loss Support Hotline—(607) 253-3932; Tuesday–Thursday 6–9 P.M. ET.
- University of Florida (no pet loss hotline, but grief counselors are available)—(352) 392-4700, then 1+4080; weekdays 7–9 P.M. ET.
- Tufts University Pet Loss Support Hotline—(508) 839-7966; Monday, Wednesday, and Thursday 6–9 P.M. ET.
- Michigan State University Pet Loss Support Hotline—(517) 432-2696; Tuesday, Wednesday, and Thursday 6:30–9:30 P.M. ET.
- Ohio State University Pet Loss Support Hotline—(614) 292-1823; Monday– Friday 6:30-9:30 P.M., Saturday 10–4 P.M. ET.
- Virginia-Maryland Regional Veterinary School Pet Loss Hotline—(540) 231-8038; Tuesday and Thursday 6–9 P.M. ET.
- The Iam's Company Pet Loss Support Hotline—(888) 332-7738; Monday–Friday 8 A.M.–5 P.M. ET.
- Florida Animal Health Foundation's Pet Grief Support Hotline—(800) 798-6196.

BURIAL OR CREMATION

Depending on your municipality, you may have a choice in how to care for your pet's remains. In most cases, you'll have the choice of a mass cremation, a private cremation, a burial at a pet cemetery, or receiving the body for burial. A mass cremation is probably the most common way of caring for a pet's remains. It is relatively inexpensive when compared to a private cremation or burial, but you do not get the remains returned to you. One crematory Maggie knows of scatters the ashes on flowerbeds. In a private cremation, you will have the remains returned to you in a box or canister (or, if you opt for it, an urn). The price of a private cremation is more than twice the cost of a mass cremation. You then have the choice of scattering your pet's remains in a favorite place or keeping the urn on a shelf.

Burial in a cemetery is probably the most expensive, depending on how elaborate you wish to make the funeral. Your pet is buried in a pet cemetery with a grave marker, and the cemetery is responsible for the upkeep of the grave. There may be a fee for keeping the grounds maintained.

Last, you may opt to bury your pet yourself. Be aware that there may be certain ordinances against burying animals on your property. Also, the place you choose should be away from where wild animals can get to the body. Sadly, Maggie once chanced on a disturbed grave along a hiking trail. Wild animals had dug up the pet's body and carried it off, leaving tufts of fur behind. We're sure that the pet owner was horrified to discover this up on his return. Don't do this.

MEMORIALS TO YOUR PET

As with humans, memorials are available to our cherished pets. There are a number of ways to remember our pets both in material and other ways. For example, many pet owners remember their pets through a donation to a favorite nonprofit organization such as a humane society or a cancer-research organization. Still others, such as The Pepper Fund, use activities that their pets enjoyed to raise funds to combat the disease that killed their pet.

Several nonprofit organizations such as the Morris Animal Foundation and the ASPCA will accept charitable donations in honor of your pet. Some shelters offer to place a plaque or memorial brick with the name of your pet if you donate a certain amount.

There are physical tributes to our pets as well. (See sidebar for listings of pet memorials). Pet urns and memorial stones or grave markers are the most common memorials, and many are listed even in pet supply catalogs.

Plaques with "The Rainbow Bridge" (page 193) inscribed can have your pet's photo and name added to them. Some people perform candle ceremonies for their pets on Monday evenings, coordinated at 10 P.M. Eastern time (see www.petloss.com for more information on the candle ceremony). Candles inscribed with a pet's name or other sentiment are available through various online retailers.

PET MEMORIALS

The following is a list of companies that provide memorial products. The companies listed are by no means exhaustive. Neither the authors nor the publisher endorse any of these products—they are included for informational purposes only.

Forever Pets
1874 Stryker Ave
St. Paul, MN 55118-4435
888-450-7727
www.foreverpets.com
Urns

Personal Creations
145 Tower Dr.
Burr Ridge, IL 60527
800-326-6626
www.personalcreations.com
Grave markers, Memorial plaques, Rainbow Bridge Plaques

The Pooka
12186 340th St
Ulen, MN 56585-9530
218-595-8360
www.thepooka.com
Rainbow Bridge Plaques

Rock-It Creations
325-C Pleasant Ave
Auburn, CA 95603
866-276-2548
www.rock-itcreations.com
Rock memorials

Whisper in the Heart
5124 Grass Valley Way
Antioch, CA, 94531
925-744-WITH
whisperintheheart.com/with
Jewelry, urn pendants

OldYeller.net Pet Memorials
Romieki Bros.
555 Fulton St. #112
San Francisco, CA 94102
415-558-9977
www.oldyeller.net
Grave markers

THE PEPPER FUND

For more information on the Pepper Memorial Classic Agility Trial, go to www.mdt-agilityability.com. To make a direct donation to the Pepper Memorial Classic Fund, contact Morris Animal Foundation at 800-243-2345 or mail to: Morris Animal Foundation, 45 Inverness Drive East, Englewood, CO 80112-5480. Please specify Pepper Memorial Classic Fund #335 on your check or when you call.

THE RAINBOW BRIDGE

Just this side of heaven is a place called Rainbow Bridge.

When an animal dies that has been especially close to someone here, that pet goes to Rainbow Bridge. There are meadows and hills for all of our special friends so they can run and play together. There is plenty of food, water, and sunshine, and our friends are warm and comfortable.

All the animals who had been ill and old are restored to health and vigor; those who were hurt or maimed are made whole and strong again, just as we remember them in our dreams of days and times gone by. The animals are happy and content, except for one small thing; they each miss someone very special, who had to be left behind.

They all run and play together, but the day comes when one suddenly stops and looks into the distance. His bright eyes are intent; His eager body quivers. Suddenly he begins to run from the group, flying over the green grass, his legs carrying him faster and faster.

You have been spotted, and when you and your special friend finally meet, you cling together in joyous reunion, never to be parted again. The happy kisses rain upon your face; your hands again caress the beloved head, and you look once more into the trusting eyes of your pet, so long gone from your life but never absent from your heart. Then you cross Rainbow Bridge together . . .

Author unknown

LETTING GO

At some point, you'll let go of the pain and start putting the sadness behind you. It starts a little at a time. You smile and laugh at something; you've stopped crying for a bit. You see another dog or cat and reach out to pet it. You find you can finally sleep through the night.

Losing a beloved pet is traumatic. How long you'll actually grieve depends a lot on you, the surprise of the death, the bond between you and your pet, and other factors. It may take days, weeks, or even months before everything seems right again. But at some point, you will need to let go and continue to live life. You can bring closure to your grief with memorials, remembrances, and perhaps talking about your pet to people who understand.

If, for whatever reason, you find that you're not bringing closure to your grief within some time, talk with a counselor or a doctor. In many instances, grief can bring prolonged depression that might need professional intervention. A professional therapist can help work with you to bring closure to your grief and your beloved pet's death.

ANOTHER DOG OR CAT?

Some people decide to get another dog or cat while their pet has cancer. The idea is to help mitigate the pain of losing the beloved pet when the time finally arrives. This can be good or bad, depending on the circumstance. If your dog or cat is used to being the only pet, he may look on this new pet as an interloper. A new dog or cat will also take a portion of your time away from your pet with cancer. If the new dog or cat is an adult, he could become aggressive with your older pet. Animals can smell when things aren't right with other animals and may "make a bid" at becoming top dog or cat.

A new puppy or kitten may alleviate that friction a bit. But be careful! A puppy or kitten will take most of your time and energy—leaving little time for your old dog or cat. Your pet with cancer may feel neglected and may become aggressive or short-tempered with your new acquisition.

However, some dogs tolerate puppies well, as some cats tolerate some kittens. Sometimes a youngster can spark new life in an old pet. Something new and exciting can shake an old dog or cat from the routine enough to make him feel young again. Some older pets are quick to become the youngster's aunt or uncle, and are delighted to "show the ropes" to the newcomer.

If you decide to get a new pet after your pet has passed on, be careful not to compare your new pet to him. It's easy to canonize a pet you've just lost even though he might not have been as perfect as you remember. When the newcomer doesn't live up to your ideal expectations ("Max never chewed up the furniture," "Princess was never this hyper!") you're likely to be overly critical of your new pet. Remember that your deceased pet might have been older, had more training, or may have been more sedate or well-behaved because he had cancer. Or you may simply remember your old pet without all the annoying faults he might have had.

Sometimes it's better to get a pet of a different color, a different breed, or even a different species. Most pets with cancer are older animals—usually housebroken or litter-box trained and less active than a new puppy or kitten. If you get a youngster, be sure you spend time with him—don't expect him to "know the ropes" the way your old pet did. Give the little guy a chance here—he doesn't know how much you've been hurting over the loss of your other pet.

Getting a new pet can help with the grieving process. No, the new pet won't ever replace your old pet. You'll always have a special place in your heart for that one dog or cat. But in time, your new pet may find a special place within your heart as well. Give him a chance and he'll show you love, too.

SUMMARY

- You should consider euthanasia if:
  - Your pet is suffering.
  - The prognosis is very poor.
  - The suffering during treatment doesn't benefit your pet.
  - You are keeping your pet alive for your sake, not his.
- There are many free grief-counseling services available for pet owners.
- There are many ways you can memorialize your pet.
- Getting another dog or cat can sometimes ease the grief.

12

Cancer on the Internet

IN THIS CHAPTER
- Learn how to determine whether the information obtained on the Internet is good or bad.
- Learn how to spot an Internet hoax.
- Learn how to evaluate a study.

When your dog or cat is sick, it's natural to want to get the most information you can about his illness. Cancer is such a dreaded disease and one that takes such a terrible toll, its one of those diseases that you'll find on the Internet. There's a lot of good information, but there's also a lot of information that's misleading, incorrect, or downright wrong. In truth, some of it ranks right up there with snake oil. Don't fall for it. During this time, you're particularly vulnerable because you're looking for something—anything—that might save your beloved pet.

Throughout this book, the authors have recommended that you work with both your veterinarian and oncologist, but we also recommend that you get as much good information as possible to make an informed decision. This information, however, needs to be reliable.

We can safely say that information you find on legitimate websites belonging to noted veterinary colleges such as Colorado State University, Tufts University, and Cornell University can be trusted to be accurate and informative. We can also recommend cancer information coming from places such as the American Veterinary Medical Association and other such organizations. However, information on these sites may be out of date due to the constant changing of cancer research and new techniques.

INTERNET HOAXES

Do you remember the old Febreze® scare? Procter and Gamble took a serious hit on the Internet when someone claimed that Febreze was dangerous to pets. Snopes.com, the Urban Legends Homepage, addresses this quite well and proves that Febreze is safe to use as directed (www.snopes.com/toxins/febreze.htm). Procter and Gamble, the makers of Febreze, also have tested their product extensively around animals, and as long as the product is used as directed, the product is safe. See (www.home madesimple.com/febreze/how_works/pet_care.shtml). The ASPCA (The American Society for the Prevention of Cruelty to Animals) furthermore endorses the product as safe when used as directed. See www.aspca.org/site/News2?page=NewsArticle&id=8352& news_iv_ctrl=-1.

So what does this mean? Before you believe anything on the Internet, you need to make certain that what you read is indeed fact. In most cases, hoaxes are scary, with little or no specific information about the cases involved. You may read something like, "A friend of mine had a dog who had cancer and she fed him turnips three times a day. After three months, the dog was cancer free." If you're savvy enough, you may notice that there's no mention of who owned this dog, what kind of cancer it was (was it even malignant?), who was the veterinarian who diagnosed the cancer, whether the dog was cured, and so on. In other words, don't start feeding your dog turnips three times a day until you get specifics and can check it out.

You can check out some urban legends at www.snopes.com.

HOW TO EVALUATE A WEBSITE

Unfortunately, anyone can put anything out on websites. A lot of what's out there is sheer trash. To determine whether the source is reputable, first look at the website itself. Who built the website, and is it a place where you can trust the information? Yes, people lie, even on websites, so don't accept a statement as being true. Is this a reputable source such as a veterinary college? Or is it someone who just has an ax to grind? Yes, even veterinarians can have unproven information on their websites, so be careful.

Question everything you see while on the Web. It may amaze you to learn that Maggie has actually heard some national radio news programs that announced information found on the Internet as being factual when in fact they were proven false. Don't believe everything you read.

Second, who put the article out? Is it a person who promises a quick fix to cancer only if you buy their product for $9.95 plus shipping and handling? Who sponsored the study? Was it a dog food company or holistic practitioner? Was it someone who has a product they're selling? While there are many unbiased studies financed by various corporations and private individuals, you still have to look hard at the study to determine if it was slanted in any way.

Third, what was the study like? How many individuals did they use? A small study with very few individuals is likely to be inconclusive; a larger study with many individuals is more likely to yield meaningful results. Also, was the study controlled adequately? For example, if you're looking at a nutrition and cancer study, were the animals fed only that specific diet in a controlled environment, or did they get treats while at home or while the owner wasn't looking?

It's tough when you're trying to figure out what course of action to take when looking on the Internet. Always question the information you find there, and don't be afraid to talk with your veterinarian and oncologist about the information you find. It may help with pet's overall prognosis.

INTERNET SITES FOR HELP WITH CANCER

The following are useful Internet sites that both Maggie and Deb have found. Be aware that these websites change frequently and we cannot vouch for the material on the websites. Use at your own risk.

1. American Academy of Veterinary Acupuncture—www.aava.org/
2. American Animal Hospital Association (AAHA)—www.aahanet.org/
3. American College of Veterinary Internal Medicine (ACVIM)—www.acvim.org/
4. American Holistic Veterinary Medication Association—www.ahvma.org/
5. American Veterinary Chiropractic Association—www.animalchiropractic.org/
6. American Veterinary Medical Association's Care for Pets—www.avma.org/care4pets/
7. Animal Cancer Foundation—www.acfoundation.org/
8. Animal Medical Center Donaldson-Atwood Cancer Clinic—www.amcny.org/department/donaldson.htm
9. Animal Medical Center in New York—www.amcny.org/

10. Argus Institute for Families and Veterinary Medicine, Colorado State University—www.argusinstitute.colostate. edu/local.htm

11. Association for Pet Loss and Bereavement—www.aplb.org

12. Colorado State University College of Veterinary Medical and Biomedical Sciences—www.cvmbs.colostate.edu/

13. Cornell University Pet Loss Support Website—web.vet. cornell.edu/public/petloss/

14. Cornell Veterinary Consultant—www.vet.cornell.edu/ consultant/consult.asp

15. CSU Animal Cancer Center—www.csuanimalcancer center.org/

16. Forever Pets—www.foreverpets.com

17. Healthy Pet (AAHA)—www.healthypet.com/

18. Holistic Medicine for Dogs and Cats—www.drnancys place.com/

19. International Association for Veterinary Homeopathy— www.iavh.at/

20. International Veterinary Acupuncture Society—www. ivas.org/

21. Memorial Sloan-Kettering Cancer Center—www.mskcc. org/mskcc/html/44.cfm

22. Morris Animal Foundation—www.morrisanimal foundation.org/

23. NetVet—http://netvet.wustl.edu/

24. Old Yeller Pet Memorials—www.oldyeller.net

25. Personal Creations—www.personalcreations.com

26. Pet Assure—www.petassure.com/

27. Pet Plan Insurance (Canada)—wwwpetplan.com/

28. PetCare Insurance Programs—www.petcareinsurance. com/us/

29. Petshealth Insurance Agency—www.petshealthplan.com/
30. Premier Pet Insurance Group—www.ppins.com/
31. Rainbow Bridge—www.alaska.net/~bearpaw/rainbow.htm
32. Rock-It Creations—www.rock-itcreations.com
33. The Animal Medical Center, Human-Animal Bond discussion group—www.amcny.org
34. The Barkley House—www.barkleyhouse.missouri.edu/
35. The Cancer Cure Foundation—www.cancure.org/pets_and_cancer.htm
36. The Pet Loss Grief Support Website—www.petloss.com
37. The Pooka—www.thepooka.com
38. The Virtual Pet Cemetery—www.lavamind.com/pet.html
39. Tuft's University School of Veterinary Medicine—www.vet.tufts.edu/
40. UC Davis School of Veterinary Medicine—www.vetmed.ucdavis.edu/
41. Veterinary Botanical Medical Association—www.vbma.org/
42. Veterinary Cancer Registry—www.vetcancerregistry.com/
43. Veterinary Cancer Society—www.vetcancersociety.org/
44. Veterinary Pet Insurance (VPI)—www.petinsurance.com/
45. Whisper In the Heart—www.whisperintheheart.com/with

SUMMARY

- Not all information on the Internet is good.
- Not all studies are completely unbiased.
- When looking at information from an unknown Internet website, regard all statements with a skeptical eye.

Glossary

adenoma—a tumor coming from epithelial cells or glands, usually benign

alimentary—referring to the digestive tract

amino acid—the building blocks of proteins

androgen—male hormone

anemia—a condition where there are not enough red blood cells

angiogenesis—the growth of new blood vessels

anorexia—lack of appetite

appendicular—referring to the limbs (legs)

ascites—fluid buildup in the abdomen

atrium—one of the two (right or left) smaller chambers of the heart

autoimmune—an immune reaction against the body's own tissues

autologous vaccines—vaccine made from a patient's own tumor antigens or cells

axial—referring to the head and the body

azotemia—an abnormal amount of urea (nitrogen waste) in the blood

benign—in cancer, this means a cancer not likely to spread to distant tissues or directly contribute to death

bile duct—small tube from the gallbladder to the intestines through which bile passes

biopsy—to remove and evaluate tissues, using a needle or surgery

body surface area—your pet's size as determined by square meters; used to determine chemotherapy dosages

bone marrow—the substance in the center of bones where blood cells are grown

bone scan—special technique to look for cancer or damage in bones, uses special dyes and imaging equipment

BUN or Blood Urea Nitrogen—the amount of urea found in a blood sample

CBC—complete blood count, used to check for anemia and white blood cell problems

CT or CAT scan—computerized axial tomography; a special type of radiography using a computer to enhance images

carcinoma—a malignant cancer from epithelial cells that tends to invade local tissues and spread to distant tissues

cardiomyopathy—a disease of the heart that either dilates or enlarges the heart muscle

carpus—the wrist, on your pet, the joint between the elbow and the paw

central nervous system—the brain and the spinal column

chemotherapy—the use of drugs to fight cancer

chronobiology—the study of changes in living things as related to the time of day

clean tissue margins—no sign of cancer cells around the edges of the biopsy specimen (done microscopically)

coagulation—clotting

cranial—to the front, but can also mean the head

cryosurgery—the use of very cold substances (such as liquid nitrogen) for surgery

cutaneous—referring to the skin

cyrptorchid—a testicle retained inside the abdomen

cystoscopy—using a special endoscope to look into the bladder

cytology—the study of cells

DIC—disseminated intravascular coagulation; uncontrolled bleeding due to all the clotting factors being used up

debulk—to reduce the size of a tumor; this can be via surgery, radiation, or chemotherapy

distal—far from the body—the distal leg could mean the paw

Doxorubicin—a chemotherapy drug, also known as Adriamycin

endoscopy—use of a small fiberoptic scope to look inside your pet

enucleation—removal of an eye

estrus—the "heat" period or time a female pet is receptive to a male and could become pregnant

FNA—fine needle aspirate; the use of a needle to draw some cells that can be evaluated under the microscope out of a growth

femur—the large bone from the hip to the knee or stifle

fine needle aspirate—see *FNA*

heat—see *estrus*

hematoma—a large blood filled mass, usually secondary to trauma

hematuria—the presence of red blood cells in the urine

hemorrhage—bleeding

hemorrhagic cystitis—a condition where the bladder's inside wall is bleeding, can lead to blood in the urine

histopathology—the science of looking at tiny tissue sections under the microscope, looking for changes or abnormalities

hock—the joint between the knee or stifle and the paw

hormones—substances made by glands that influence other parts of the body

humerus—the large bone between the shoulder and the elbow

hypercalcemia—abnormally high levels of calcium in the blood

hyperplasia—excessive growth of a tissue

hyperthermy—the use of heat to treat growths

hyphema—blood in the front part of the eye

hypocalcemia—abnormally low levels of calcium in the blood

icterus—yellowish pigment in tissues, jaundice; usually due to bile or damaged red blood cells

induction—the start of chemotherapy treatment, aiming at remission

inflammatory carcinoma—a cancer with large numbers of inflammatory cells, a very reactive cancer

insulinoma—a cancer that produces insulin

intralesional—occurring within the lesion or defect; often refers to giving a treatment directly into the abnormal tissues

intraoperative—occurring during surgery; intraoperative radiation is radiation treatment given during surgery

intravascular—occurring within blood vessels

jaundice—yellowish pigment in tissues, icterus; usually due to bile or damaged red blood cells

lifetime maximum dose—the "safe" amount of a chemotherapy drug or radiation that can be given without dangerous side effects

limb sparing—surgical technique whereby the surgeon tries to save most of the leg by special techniques including bone grafts; an alternative to amputation for some bone cancer patients

lymph node—solid areas of lymphatic tissue located throughout the body, which drain lymph and fluids from tissues; involved directly in lymphomas and indirectly in many other cancers as sites for metastasis

lytic—destructive, often refers to cancers that destroy bone

MDB—minimum data base, the base knowledge that your veterinarian will want to diagnose your pet's cancer and help plan a course of treatment

MRI—magnetic resonance imaging; use of magnets, a computer and radio waves to evaluate tissues

MTP-PE—an adjuvant used to stimulate immune responses

maintenance—in cancer treatment, this refers to the separate dosaging schedule for chemotherapy or radiation to keep a cancer under control

malignant—a cancer that invades local tissues aggressively and usually spreads to distant tissues via metastases; it can also mean certain cellular characteristics

mammary chain—the chain of breast tissue along the body wall in dogs and cats

mastitis—inflammation and/or infection of the mammary tissues

mediastinum—the area between the lungs

meninges—the tissue covering over the brain and the spinal cord

metastasis—the spread of cancer to distant tissues, usually a sign of malignancy

mitosis—the reproductive cycle of cells

mitotic index—the rate at which cells are dividing/reproducing

multicentric—describes a cancer with two or more separate tumors

musculoskeletal—referring to the muscles and bones of the body

myelodepression—damage to the bone marrow, leading to decreased production of blood cells

nanobiology—the study of very small living organisms such as individual cells

neurologic—referring to nervous tissue or the nervous system

ocular—referring to the eye

oncologist—a specialist in the medicine of cancer—diagnosing and treating it

open cell polylactic acid—phosphorus plus a biodegradable polymer

oral—referring to the mouth

organophosphate—chemical substances composed of alcohols and phosphoric acid; used primarily in pesticides

osteomyelitis—inflammation/infection of bone

pancreas—an organ that produces insulin and many digestive enzymes, located near the intestines

papilloma—a small benign tumor, sometimes associated with a virus

paraneoplastic syndrome—a syndrome associated with, but not necessarily directly caused by, a cancer—for example, increased calcium in the blood with lymphoma

paresis—partial paralysis

pathologist—a scientist who studies tissues, looking for disease

perianal—occurring around the anus

photodynamic—use of light and a photosensitizing substance

physiologic—referring to how tissues and organs work and their functions

platelets—small pieces of large cells called thrombocytes that help in the clotting of blood

prescapular—in front of the shoulder

progestins—steroid hormones that act like progesterone

protocol—a schedule of chemotherapy treatment

pyometra—an infection of the uterus

radiation—use of special energy waves to treat or diagnose cancer

radiographs—commonly referred to as "x-rays"; the images made by using radiation to evaluate a patient

radius—one of the long bones in the forearm, between the elbow and the carpus or wrist

remission—the disappearance of cancer; this could be permanent (cure) or more commonly, temporary

retroperitoneal—located in the abdomen, up along the spine, near the kidneys

sarcoma—a cancer that develops in connective tissue (such as bone), often malignant

scintigraphy—the use of radioisotopes to look at and evaluate tissues

spay—to remove the uterus and ovaries

spleen—an organ in the abdomen where blood is produced, filtered, and stored

squamous—flat cells that line many organs and form the outer layer of the skin (scalelike)

stifle—the knee or joint between the hip and the hock on the hind leg

sublumbar—below the lumbar (lower back) area

submandibular—below the lower jaw

Tamoxifen—an anti-estrogen drug

telomerase—an enzyme involved in the reproduction of cells

thoracic—referring to the chest

tibia—one of the long bones from the stifle to the hock

trematode—a class of parasites

ureters—the tubes that lead from the kidneys to the bladder

urinalysis—diagnostic evaluation of urine

urinary tract—the organs and tissues involved in urine production and removal; the kidneys, ureters, bladder, and urethra.

uvea—a vascular layer of the eye

vascular—having many blood vessels

vulvar—around the vulva (urinary and genital opening) of a female dog or cat

x-ray—see *radiograph*

Sources

1. *Small Animal Clinical Oncology* by S. Withrow, DVM, and E.G. MacEwen, VMD. W. B. Saunders, 1996.
2. *Cancer in Dogs and Cats* by W. Morrison, DVM, MS. Teton NewMedia. 2002.
3. *Feline Oncology* by G. Ogilvie, DVM, and A. Moore, MVSc. Veterinary Learning Systems. 2001.
4. *Comp of Cont Ed. 26*(4), 4/04. "MRI in Small Animal Medicine: Clinical Applications" by Hosman A. Pooya, DVM, et al.
5. *Comp of Cont Ed. 26*(4) 4/04. "Dactinomycin" by Louis-Phillipe de Lorinier, DVM, and Barbara E. Kitchel, DVM, Ph.D., DACVIM.
6. http://www.vin.com/VINDBPub/SerachPB/Proceedings/PRO 5000/PRO0484.htm. "A Systemic Approach to Cancer in Pets: Clinical Evaluation and Staging" by Margaret C. McEntee, DVM, DACVIM, DACVR.
7. http://www.mediarelations.ksu.edu/WEB/News?NewsReleases/ listpetcare62502.html. "CT, MRI and Radiation Therapy."

8. http://www.hat.org.uk/fsheets/fsheets2.html.

9. *Comp. Of Cont Ed., 26*(1) 1/04."Liver Tumors in Cats and Dogs" by Julius M. Lipstak BVSc, MVetClinStud, FACVS, et al.

10. CNYVMA Newsletter, Spring 2004. "Radiation Therapy Facts from Cornell."

11. Radiation notes from continuing education meeting, Cornell, by Margaret McEntee, DVM.

12. *Vet. Radiol. and Ultrasound, 43*(5), 2002. "Preoperative radiotherapy for vaccine associated sarcoma in 92 cats" Tetsuya Kobayaski, DVM, et al.

13. *Vet. Prac News*, 6/04. "How Cancer Causes Anemia" by Alice Villalobos, DVM.

14. *Cancer, Pets and People*, brochure, Cornell Veterinary College.

15. *Cornell University Veterinary Medicine Newsletter,* Fall 2002.

16. *Vet Prac. News*, 2/04. "Oral Cancer Mimics Dental Disease," by Alice Villalobos, DVM.

17. AJVR, *65*(2), Feb 2004. "Isolation, characterization and expression of feline stromolysin-1 in naturally developing tumors in cats" by Kara C. Sorenson, Ph.D., et al.

18. JAVMA, *224*(9), May 2004. "Retroperitoneal sarcomas in dogs: 14 cases (1992–2002)" by Julius M. Liptak, BVSc, MVetClinStud, et al.

19. *Comp of Cont Ed. 25*(8), Aug 2003. "Canine Lymphosarcoma: An In Depth Look" by Ravinder S. Dhaliwal, DVM, MS, et al.

20. *Comp of Cont Ed. 26*(6), June 2004. "Melphalan" by Amy L. Weidermann, DVM, et al.

21. *Natural Health Bible for Dogs & Cats: You're A–Z Guide to Over 200 Conditions, Herbs, Vitamins and Supplements* by Shawn Messonnier, DVM. New York: Three Rivers Press, 2001.

22. *Why Is Cancer Killing our Pets?* by Deborah Straw. Rochester, VT: Healing Arts Press, 2000.

23. http://clincancerres.aacrjournals.org/cgi/content/full/7/3/65. "Photodynamic Therapy in the Canine Prostate Using Motexafin Lutetium" by R. Alex Hsi et al.

24. *Veterinary and Comparative Oncology 1*(1), 48–56, 2003.

25. "Immunohistochemical characterization of canine prostatic carcinoma and correlation with castration status and castration time" by K. U. Sorenmo, M. Goldschmidt, F. Shofer, C. Goldkamp, and J. Ferracone.

26. http://www.angio.org/pets_and_wildlife/pet/cancer_canine.html.

27. Cornell Feline Health Center.

28. *Managing the Veterinary Cancer Patient* by G. Ogilvie, DVM, and A. Moore, MVSc. Veterinary Learning Systems, 1995.

29. www.avma.org/vafstf.

30. http://www.gcvs.com/oncology.

31. http://www.pamf.org/health/guidelines/geneticscreening.html.

32. http://www.labbies.com/cancer.

33. *Vet Pathol 41*, (2004), 209–214 © 2004 American College of Veterinary Pathologists, p. 53. "Expression and Environmental Tobacco Smoke Exposure in Feline Oral Squamous Cell Carcinoma" by L. A. Snyder, E. R. Bertone, R. M. Jakowski, M. S. Dooner, J. Jennings-Ritchie, and A. S. Moore.

34. http://www.vin.com/VINDBPub/SearchPB/Proceedings/PRO5000/PR00390.htm. "Current Management Recommendations for Canine Mast Cell Tumors" by Margaret C. McEntee, DVM, DACVIM (oncology), DACVR (radiation oncology), Cornell University.

35. http://www.vet.upenn.edu/departments/csp/oncology.

36. http://www.winnfelinehealth.org/health/hyperthyroidism.html—article by Dr. Susan Little, DVM, Dipl ABVP (Feline).

37. *Pet Care in The New Century* by Amy D. Shojai. New York: New American Library, 2001.

38. *Pets Living with Cancer* by Robin Downing, DVM. Englewood, CO: AHAA Press, 2000.

39. *The Complete Idiot's Guide to Dog Health and Nutrition* by Margaret H. Bonham, and James M. Wingert, DVM. Indianapolis: Alpha Books, 2003.

40. *The Holistic Dog Book*, by Denise Flaim. Hoboken, NJ: Howell Book House, 2003.

41. Morris Animal Foundation, Heidi Jeter, et al.

42. Conversations with Dr. Phillip Bergman, head of the Donaldson-Atwood Cancer Center and diplomate of ACVIM.

43. Conversations with Dr. David Vail, DVM.

44. Conversations with Dr. Carol Henry, DVM.

45. Conversations with Dr. Alan Schoen, DVM.

46. *Veterinarians Guide to Natural Remedies for Dogs: Safe and Effective Alternative Treatments and Healing Techniques from the Nation's Top Holistic Veterinarians* by Martin Zucker. New York: Three Rivers Press, 2000.

47. *Dr. Pitcairn's Complete Guide to Natural Health for Dogs & Cats* by Richard H. Pitcairn, DVM, Ph.D., and Susan Hubble Pitcairn. Emmaus, PA: Rodale Books, 1995.

48. *The Dog Owner's Home Veterinary Handbook*, 3rd ed. by James M. Giffin, M.D., and Liisa D Carlson, DVM. New York: Howell Book House, 2000.

49. *The Cat Owner's Home Veterinary Handbook by* Delbert G Carlson, DVM, James M Giffin, M.D., and Liisa D. Carlson, DVM. New York: Howell Book House, 1995.

50. The American Veterinary Medical Association, www.avma.org.

51. *The Dog Repair Book* by Ruth B. James, DVM. Mills, WY: Alpine Press, 1990.

52. *The Complete Book of Dog Care* by Ulrich Klever. Hauppauge, NY: Barron's Educational Series, 1989.

53. *The Merck Veterinary Manual, Seventh Ed.* Whitehouse Station, NJ: Merck and Co, Inc., 1991.

54. Conversations with Dr. Rebecca Remillard, Ph.D., DVM, DACVN, veterinary nutritionist and past president of the American Academy of Veterinary Nutritionists. Angell Animal Medical Center, Boston.

55. Winn Feline Health Foundation, www.winnfelinehealth.org.

56. AKC Canine Health Foundation, www.akcchf.org.

57. Conversations with Dr. Christine Chambreau, DVM.

58. Conversations with Dr. H.C. Gurney, DVM.

Index